August Wilson's
Two Trains Running

D0833097

A SAMUEL FRENCH ACTING EDITION

SAMUEL
FRENCH
FOUNDED 1830

SAMUELFRENCH.COM
SAMUELFRENCH-LONDON.CO.UK

FOR PRODUCTION ENQUIRIES

UNITED STATES AND CANADA
Info@SamuelFrench.com
1-866-598-8449

UNITED KINGDOM AND EUROPE
Plays@SamuelFrench-London.co.uk
020-7255-4302

Each title is subject to availability from Samuel French, depending upon country of performance. Please be aware that *TWO TRAINS RUNNING* may not be licensed by Samuel French in your territory. Professional and amateur producers should contact the nearest Samuel French office or licensing partner to verify availability.

MUSIC USE NOTE

Licensees are solely responsible for obtaining formal written permission from copyright owners to use copyrighted music in the performance of this play and are strongly cautioned to do so. If no such permission is obtained by the licensee, then the licensee must use only original music that the licensee owns and controls. Licensees are solely responsible and liable for all music clearances and shall indemnify the copyright owners of the play(s) and their licensing agent, Samuel French, against any costs, expenses, losses and liabilities arising from the use of music by licensees. Please contact the appropriate music licensing authority in your territory for the rights to any incidental music.

IMPORTANT BILLING AND CREDIT REQUIREMENTS

If you have obtained performance rights to this title, please refer to your licensing agreement for important billing and credit requirements.

TWO TRAINS RUNNING opened at the Yale Repertory Theatre (Lloyd Richards, Artistic Director; Benjamin Mordecai, Managing Director) on March 27, 1990 in New Haven, Connecticut. It was directed by Lloyd Richards with set design by Tony Fanning, costume design by Chrisi Karvonides, lighting design by Geoff Korf, sound design by Ann Johnson and production dramaturgy by Lisa A. Wilde. The Production Stage Manager was Liz Dreyer. The cast was as follows:

MEMPHIS	Al White
WOLF	Samuel L. Jackson
RISA	Ella Joyce
HOLLOWAY	Samuel E. Wright
STERLING	Laurence Fishburne
HAMBONE	Sullivan Walker
WEST	Leonard Parker

TWO TRAINS RUNNING opened at the Walter Kerr Theatre on Broadway in New York City on April 13, 1992. The Executive Producer was Benjamin Mordecai. It was directed by Lloyd Richards with set design by Tony Fanning, costume design by Chrisi Karvonides, and lighting design by Geoff Korf. The Production Stage Manager was Karen L. Carpenter and the Stage Manager was Fred Seagraves. The cast was as follows:

MEMPHIS	Al White
WOLF	Anthony Chisholm
RISA	Cynthia Martells
HOLLOWAY	Roscoe Lee Browne
STERLING	Laurence Fishburne
HAMBONE	Sullivan Walker
WEST	Chuck Patterson

CHARACTERS

MEMPHIS

WOLF

RISA

HOLLOWAY

STERLING

HAMBONE

WEST

< 1929

built 1939

SETTING

It is Pittsburgh, 1969. The action of the play takes place in a restaurant across the street from West's Funeral Home and Lutz's Meat Market. It is a small restaurant with four stools, a counter, a pay phone, and three booths lined against one wall. The menu is printed on a blackboard behind the counter.

coffee pot

the hill district

a variation of bronzeville

tail end of economic viability

Some way to look out – window

Step up to the door

Cash register

love & death

love & loss

This one's for Judy

If the train don't hurry
there's gonna be some walking done.
-Traditional

ACT ONE

Scene I

(The lights come up on the restaurant. The menu reads:)

> Beans w/corn muffins .65¢
> Chicken w/2 sides $2.45
> Meatloaf w/2 sides $2.35
> Sides:
>> Collard greens
>> Mashed potatoes
>> Green beans
>> Macaroni & cheese
>> Potato salad

*(The winning number combination of the previous day, 651, is also written on the menu board. **WOLF** is in the telephone booth. He comes out, shuffles some papers, and starts to his seat at the counter when the phone rings. He answers it just as **MEMPHIS** enters from the back carrying a newspaper. **MEMPHIS** is a self-made man whose values of hard work, diligence, persistence, and honesty have been consistently challenged by the circumstances of his life. His greatest asset is his impeccable logic. **WOLF**, on the phone, writes something down.)*

WOLF. Wolf... Eight sixty-four. Boxed for a dollar... Yeah, I got that.

MEMPHIS. Hey Wolf, I told you about that. You can't be tying up my phone with them numbers.

WOLF. Seven thirty-one straight...for a dollar. Okay.

(**WOLF** *hangs up and exits the phone booth. He is a man who enjoys his notoriety and popularity as the community's numbers runner. While he manages to keep money in his pocket and a decent pair of shoes on his feet, his inability to find secure female companionship is the single failure that marks his life.*)

MEMPHIS. I told you about tying up my phone with them numbers. I don't want that in here.

WOLF. Who's trying to call you? Risa will tell you...ain't nobody trying to call you.

MEMPHIS. My lawyer might be trying to call me.

WOLF. That's what happened to Harvey before he got them ten years. He sitting around waiting for his lawyer to call him. If I was him I would have been in Cleveland or Detroit. Naw, he wanna sit around and wait on his lawyer to call him.

MEMPHIS. This a civil lawyer. There's more than one kind of lawyer. But you don't know nothing about that.

WOLF. I know there's different kinds of lawyers. The NAACP got all kinds of lawyers. It don't do nobody no good. *(calls out)* Hey, Risa, give me some sugar.

MEMPHIS. That's the second time this week that six fifty-one hit. I don't know the last time I can recall a number coming twice in the same week. That was L. D.'s number. If he was still living he'd be in big money.

WOLF. They had that six ninety-four come twice about a year ago. Milt hit for five dollars both times. Got mad 'cause he didn't have twenty dollars on it. *(calls)* Let me get some sugar, Risa.

(**RISA** *enters from the back.* **RISA** *is a young woman who, in an attempt to define herself in terms other than her genitalia, has scarred her legs with a razor.*)

MEMPHIS. I remember that. I had six ninety-six. I switched off to six ninety-two and it come back six ninety-four. I remember that. You talk about Milt being mad.

RISA. I don't know why people waste their money playing numbers. Time you hit you just getting back what you put in.

WOLF. It's the same thing as putting money in the bank. This way you might take out more than you put in... but Mellon ain't gonna let you do that. The numbers give you an opportunity. If it wasn't for the numbers all these niggers would be poor.

MEMPHIS. It wasn't till I hit the numbers eight or nine years ago that I got to the point where I could change my clothes every day. See, most of these niggers around here can't do that. The only way they can do that is to hit the numbers or get lucky in a crap game. The ones that working... the only way they can do anything is to wait on their income tax return. Half the time the government cheat them out of that.

WOLF. You hear from your old lady, Memphis?

MEMPHIS. Don't bring up that woman to me. I ain't heard from her. I know where she at. She up her sister's house. She been up there them two months since she left. Twenty-two years. I give her everything I had for twenty-two years. Naw...naw...I give her everything I had when I met her...then I give her everything I could get hold of for the next twenty-two years. And then when she was leaving...she wouldn't even shake my hand.

WOLF. I know how that go. That's why I don't mess with these women but so far.

MEMPHIS. I ain't never left nobody in bad manners. I'm standing there trying to say "May God bless you everywhere you go"...and she wouldn't even shake my hand.

RISA. Maybe she didn't like the way you was treating her.

MEMPHIS. I treat that woman like she was a queen. Treat her like she made out of gold. Try to give her everything she want. She say, "Baby I want a car," she got a Cadillac. She want a TV…she got a color TV. It might take me a little while. Her wants might be too big for my pocket but I work it out and come up with something. I was working on the dishwasher when she walked out. I would have got her that but the plumbing got to be right. I'm talking to John D. about him fixing up the plumbing…and she got up and walked out the door. You talking about she tired of the way I treated her. I treated that woman like she was the Queen of Sheba.

RISA. Maybe she don't see it like that. She had to leave for something.

MEMPHIS. I ain't done nothing but ask her to get up and make me some bread. And she got up and walked out the door. I know she don't expect me to make it myself. Got up and walked out the door! I went down there and saw her. Asked her what the matter was. She told me she was tired. Now, how you gonna get more tired than I am? I'm the one going out there wrestling with the world. She ain't got to do nothing but stay home and take care of the house. She got it nice. Talking about she tired. She wasn't too tired to make them four babies.

> (**HOLLOWAY** enters. **HOLLOWAY** is a man who all his life has voiced his outrage at injustice with little effect. His belief in the supernatural has enabled him to accept his inability to effect change and continue to pursue life with zest and vigor.)

HOLLOWAY. Hey, Wolf.

WOLF. What's happening, Holloway?

HOLLOWAY. The people lined up all the way up there past Webster to see Prophet Samuel. They was lined up there before the doors open. West ain't had a chance to open his door good before they was all tramping through there. They got a line all the way up past Webster. They done had two fellows get in a fight about gypping the line.

WOLF. Where?

HOLLOWAY. Just now as I was coming down. Man tried to slide in there beside somebody he knew and got in a fight about it.

WOLF. I knew it was gonna be crowded. I didn't know they would be lined up.

HOLLOWAY. Lined clear up to Webster. It take you an hour to get in there to see him.

WOLF. They say how he died?

MEMPHIS. Ask Risa. She should know. She running up there giving the man her money.

HOLLOWAY. They say he had a stroke.

MEMPHIS. I believe one of them old sandal-foot woman poisoned him. I wouldn't be a bit surprised. Got all them women walking around his house together... I wouldn't be a bit surprised if one of them didn't get jealous and poison him.

HOLLOWAY. They over there now greeting the people and falling all over the place. All seven or eight of them. West can't wait to bury that nigger. One of them wanted to charge the people to see him, but West wouldn't have that over there. You think I'm lying, don't you? They had a little basket they put over there right by the casket. They was charging people a dollar to see him before West put a stop to it.

MEMPHIS. When they gonna bury him?

WOLF. Tuesday. They say they gonna bury him Tuesday.

HOLLOWAY. They gonna try and bury him Tuesday. West ain't gonna bury him until the people got a chance to see him.

WOLF. They say he got hundred-dollar bills in the casket with him.

HOLLOWAY. He got hundred-dollar bills…got diamonds on all his fingers. They got it roped off. You can't get within ten feet of the casket. He got gold and jewels and everything in there with him.

WOLF. What…they supposed to bury him with all that money?

MEMPHIS. West ain't gonna bury that man with that money. West ain't no fool. You think he gonna put money and diamonds and all that gold in the ground? Half the time he don't even put the casket. Half the time he dump the body out and bring the casket back to sell it again. Bury somebody else in it.

RISA. West don't be doing that. That's against the law.

HOLLOWAY. West done buried four or five niggers in the same suit. How you think he got all that money?

WOLF. Who would you say had the most money – West or Prophet Samuel?

HOLLOWAY. Everybody know West got money. He get more business. More people dying than getting saved.

WOLF. Prophet Samuel got a lot of money. He right up there with West. He be cheating and fooling the people all these years.

RISA. He ain't done nothing but tell the truth. Most times people don't want to hear the truth. But Prophet Samuel say the truth ain't nothing to be afraid of. He say if you afraid of the truth to get back in the shadows 'cause you never will see the light.

WOLF. I ain't said all that. I just said he right up there with West when it comes to money. All them jewels and things he had. That big old white Cadillac. Seven or eight women. He was living a nice life.

MEMPHIS. He ain't got nothing now. He ain't got as much as you got. And I don't believe he had as much money as West. West got money he ain't even counted.

WOLF. How much money would you say he got?

HOLLOWAY. West got a million dollars. Got it two or three times.

MEMPHIS. And don't know how to spend it. Man living up over top of the funeral home – you'd think he'd have enough sense to buy him a house somewhere. He own every other building around here. Them that Hartzberger don't own. I got lucky and got hold to this piece of building and West got mad. I got it right out from under his nose and he ain't never forget that. All that property he own and had the nerve to get mad when I bought this. What make it so bad is he could have had it. He was talking to L.D. about buying the building from him. L.D. had his stroke and West figured he'd wait until he died and get it cheaper. I went over to the hospital to see him and we made the deal right there in the hospital about a week before he died. I got it for fifty-five hundred dollars. This is when I was walking around with four or five hundred dollars in my pocket every day. Used to carry a pistol and everything. Had me a forty-four. Had me one of them big forty-fours. Used to scare me to look at it. I give L.D. the fifty-five hundred in cash. I didn't find out till after he died that he owed twelve hundred dollars in back taxes...but I didn't care. I had seen a way for me to take off my pistol. I got my deed and went right home... took off my pistol and hung it up in the closet. West got mad when he found out L.D. sold me the building. He been trying to buy it from me ever since. He walked in the next day and offered me eight thousand dollars for it. That was a good price. But see...he didn't know it had come to mean more to me than that. I had found a way to live the rest of my life.

WOLF. When they gonna tear it down?

HOLLOWAY. You know how the city is. They been gonna tear this whole block down for the last twenty years.

MEMPHIS. They told me to be downtown Tuesday. They liable to wait another twenty years before they tear it down, but I'm supposed to be down there Tuesday and find out how much they gonna give me.

WOLF. What you gonna do when they tear it down?

MEMPHIS. Ain't nothing to do. Unless I do like West and go into the undertaking business. I can't go out there in Squirrel Hill and open up a restaurant. Ain't nothing gonna be left around here. Supermarket gone. Two drugstores. The five and ten. Doctor done moved out. Dentist done moved out. Shoe store gone. Ain't nothing gonna be left but these niggers killing one another. That don't never go out of style. West gonna get richer and everybody else gonna get poorer. At one time you couldn't get a seat in here. Had the jukebox working and everything. Time somebody get up somebody sit down before they could get out the door. People coming from everywhere. Everybody got to eat and everybody got to sleep. Some people don't have stoves. Some people don't have nobody to cook for them. Men whose wives done died and left them. Cook for them thirty years and lay down and die. Who's gonna cook for them now? Somebody got to do it. I order four cases of chicken on Friday and Sunday it's gone. Fry it up. Make a stew. Boil it. Add some dumplings. You couldn't charge more than a dollar. But then you didn't have to. It didn't cost you but a quarter. People used to come from all over. The man used to come twice a week to collect the jukebox. He making more money than I am. He pay seventy-five cents for the record and he make two hundred dollars off it. If it's a big hit he's liable to make four hundred. The record will take all the quarters you can give it. It don't never wear out. The chicken be gone by Sunday. It ain't nothing like that now. I'm lucky if I go through a case a chicken a week. That's all right. I'll take that. I ain't greedy. But if they wanna tear it down they gonna have to meet my price.

WOLF. They ought to give you a good price. That's what I hear...when the city buy something they give you a good price.

MEMPHIS. They give white folks a good price. Most time that be who they buying it from. Well, they gonna give me just like they give them. I bought it eight years ago for fifty-five hundred dollars and I ain't taking a penny less than twenty-five thousand.

WOLF. You ought to be able to get that.

MEMPHIS. Let me get a dollar on that seven sixty-four. If that come out that'll hold me till the city do their paperwork. If that come out I might buy me a new pair of shoes. I ain't going to be like West. West been wearing the same pair of shoes for three years. Got the heels all run over and everything. He do keep them shined. I'll say that for him. I ain't never seen him without his shoes shined.

WOLF. I ain't never seen him without them gloves. He wear them gloves everywhere. I believe he wear them to bed. I hear tell he got a wooden hand.

HOLLOWAY. West ain't got no wooden hand. He be touching them dead people... I'd wear gloves too.

WOLF. He can take them off and wash his hands. He don't be touching them all the time. I ain't never seen him without them gloves. I ain't never seen him in nothing but black. Everything he wear is black. Black hat. Black suit. Black shoes. Black tie. The only thing he wear is that white shirt. Everything else is black.

HOLLOWAY. That's what he supposed to wear. All undertakers wear black. What it look like if he showed up to bury somebody in a red suit? They supposed to wear black.

WOLF. He do make them bodies look good. Make them look natural.

MEMPHIS. People kill me with that. How somebody dead gonna look natural?

WOLF. That's what the people say. Say they look better than when they was living. That's why the people like West.

HOLLOWAY. The people like West 'cause he get the cars there on time. He say he be there to pick you up at one o'clock...that's what time he come. He be real nice and polite – it's "No, sir" and "Yes, ma'am." "Watch your step." "Can I get you some water?" The people like that. You even act like you want to faint and West will be right there at your elbow.

MEMPHIS. He do all that after he got the money.

HOLLOWAY. Quite naturally he gonna get the money first.

MEMPHIS. You go over there looking for a pine box and walk out with a five-thousand-dollar silver, satin-lined casket, guaranteed to be leak-proof. That's what get me. For an extra hundred dollars he give you a twenty-year guarantee that the casket ain't gonna leak and let the water seep in. Now how dumb can anybody get? You gonna dig up the casket twenty years later to see if it's leaking and go back and tell West and get your hundred dollars back? The first time it rain the water's liable to drown the corpse. You don't know. Yet you be surprised at the number of people come out of there talking about their twenty-year guarantee. Then if that ain't enough he charge you another hundred dollars to get a casket that lock. Like somebody gonna go down there and steal the body if it ain't locked up. Yet they come out of there clutching this little key he give them. West the only nigger I know who can cheat and rob the people and they be happy to see him. Calling him "Mr. West." "How you doing, Mr. West?" "Have a nice day, Mr. West." "Good to see you, Mr. West." He done cheated them out of four or five hundred dollars and they talking about, "Have a nice day, Mr. West."

WOLF. I don't want West to bury me. I'll go anywhere else. Charles. McTurner. Harris. I'll let anybody bury me but West. Hell, I'm liable to do like the white folks do and get cremated.

MEMPHIS. What you got against West?

WOLF. I ain't got nothing against him. I just don't want him standing over me when I'm dead. I'd rather have a stranger standing over me.

HOLLOWAY. You ain't gonna know nothing about it. What you care who be standing over top of you? You talk foolish. West don't care nothing about you. The last person West buried that he cared about was his wife. He don't care nothing about you. You just be another dead nigger to him. I doubt if West can tell one nigger from another. Man got four or five viewing rooms and don't have no trouble keeping somebody in all of them. I remember one time he had two niggers laid out in the hallway and one on the back porch. Most of them had welfare caskets, but West don't care 'cause the government pay on time. He might have to worry his money out of some of them other niggers, but the government pay quicker than the insurance companies.

MEMPHIS. Wasn't nothing but a pine box with some cloth stretched over it. That's what the welfare casket was.

WOLF. They ain't changed. That's what they is now.

> (HAMBONE *enters. He is in his late forties. He is self-contained and in a world of his own. His mental condition has deteriorated to such a point that he can only say two phrases, and he repeats them idiotically over and over.*)

HAMBONE. He gonna give me my ham. He gonna give me my ham. I want my ham. He gonna give me my ham.

RISA. Hambone, where you been? What I tell you? It don't matter whether you got any money or not...you come and get something to eat. You hear?

HAMBONE. He gonna give me my ham. He gonna give me my ham.

RISA. How you been? You been doing all right?

> (RISA *fixes him a bowl of beans and some cornbread. She sets it in front of him.*)

HAMBONE. He gonna give me my ham. He gonna give me my ham.

RISA. You go on and eat. I got something for you.

> (RISA *exits into the back.*)

HAMBONE. He gonna give me my ham.

MEMPHIS. All right, that's enough of that now!

HAMBONE. *(under his breath)* I want my ham. He gonna give me my ham.

> *(**RISA** comes out with a wool sport coat. She gives it to **HAMBONE**.)*

RISA. Here…put this on. It be cold out there sometimes at night. You button it up too.

WOLF. Risa, you been over to see Prophet Samuel yet? I know you going over.

RISA. I ain't going. I don't want to see him like that.

MEMPHIS. Risa been around here crying for two days. I tried to tell her the man got to die sometime.

WOLF. Ain't nothing to it. Ain't nothing but a dead body laying up there.

RISA. That's what I know. That's why I don't want to go.

WOLF. Ain't nothing to be scared of. I done seen a whole bunch of dead niggers.

MEMPHIS. You around here following the man. Running up there giving the man your money, talking about Prophet Samuel this, Prophet Samuel that…and now you don't want to go pay your respect.

WOLF. Risa…I'll go over with you any time you wanna go. Here…put that in the jukebox. *(hands **RISA** two quarters)*

RISA. It's broke.

WOLF. I thought it was just fixed. Memphis, I thought you was gonna get you a new jukebox.

MEMPHIS. I told Zanelli to bring me a new one. That what he say he gonna do. He been saying that for the last year. *(pause)* Risa, get on back there and get that chicken ready, you ain't got time to be standing around.

> *(**RISA** exits into the back. **MEMPHIS** takes his papers and goes to the booth.)*

> *(**STERLING** enters. He is a young man of thirty. He wears a suit and a dress shirt without a tie, along with a straw hat that is out of style. He has*

*been out of the penitentiary for one week and the
suit is his prison issue.* **STERLING** *appears at times
to be unbalanced, but it is a combination of his
unorthodox logic and straightforward manner that
makes him appear so.)*

MEMPHIS. *(cont.) (calling)* Hey, Risa.

*(**RISA** enters from the back.)*

RISA. What?

MEMPHIS. What you mean, "What?" You see the man sitting there... Wait on him. That's what you here for.

RISA. I was trying to clean the chicken.

MEMPHIS. The man want to eat now. He ain't thinking about you cleaning no chicken.

RISA. We ain't got no chicken. And we ain't got no meat loaf. We ain't got no hamburger either. We just got beans and cornbread.

MEMPHIS. You got some hamburger back there.

RISA. It's all frozen.

MEMPHIS. Well, take it out the freezer, thaw it out. Don't tell the man you ain't got none. Tell him you forgot to thaw it out.

RISA. You want some beans?

STERLING. That's all you got is beans? I don't want no beans. I been eating beans for five years. You got a great big sign out there say "restaurant" and you ain't got no food. Where your menu? You got a menu? What that say up there? "Meat loaf with greens and mash potatoes." Give me some meat loaf. Some collard greens. You got all that sign out there say home-style cooking. Where the food at?

MEMPHIS. You got to come back, I ain't went shopping yet. She have some chicken in a minute. Risa, go on back in there and get on that chicken. You been back there for a half hour and ain't even got the grease in the pan. *(to* **STERLING***)* She'll fry you up some chicken in a minute. She got the rice on.

RISA. I told you ain't but a half a box of rice.

MEMPHIS. Well, cook that up. That's better than nothing.

STERLING. You ought to put a sign out there. Say: "Gone shopping." Say, baby, give me a cup of coffee.

MEMPHIS. Go on and give him some coffee and get on back to frying up that chicken before somebody else come in here.

RISA. You want cream?

STERLING. I like it black.

(**RISA** *pours him a coffee.*)

Oh, I know you. I know who you are.

RISA. Oh, yeah?

STERLING. You Rodney's sister. What happened? Where you get them hips from? You used to be a little skinny old thing. You don't remember me? Sterling Johnson. Used to be with Rodney all the time? You don't remember me? That's all right, I remember you.

MEMPHIS. Risa, get on back there and get to work. You ain't got time to be standing around talking.

STERLING. This an old friend of mine. I knew her before you did. Her name is Clarissa Thomas. She got a brother named Rodney.

MEMPHIS. I don't care how long you known her. She working now. She can't be standing around talking. She got things to do.

STERLING. Say, baby, if you get fired I can't take care of you. I'm trying to find a job myself. I just got out the penitentiary.

RISA. I ain't worried about getting fired.

STERLING. Where's Rodney staying? I kinda got out of touch with him.

RISA. He moved to Cleveland. He said he had to get out of Pittsburgh before he kill somebody.

STERLING. Me and him had some fun times together. You remember I used to come up to the house and eat all the time? That was you that was doing all the cooking. Rodney say, "Come on, man, my sister got something to eat." Then we used to come up there. You used to be skinny.

RISA. I wasn't all that skinny.

STERLING. I don't know how skinny you were but you sure grown up now. What's your phone number?

RISA. I ain't got none.

STERLING. Well, what's the address? If I can't walk I'll crawl up there.

MEMPHIS. Risa, get on back there and get that chicken fried up so you can go get West his pie before he be over here.

RISA. I'm frying it!

(RISA exits into the back.)

STERLING. *(almost to himself)* Seem like to me if you come to work all the time and can't talk to nobody, then I don't know who would want that job. It's like being in school with somebody always telling you what to do. *(to WOLF)* How you doing? I seen you down at Irv's.

WOLF. Yeah, I be down there sometimes.

STERLING. I just got out the penitentiary. I was down at Irv's yesterday. But I figure I hang out down there I'll be right back down the penitentiary. I don't want that. I'm trying to find a job. You know where I can get a job? Anybody know where I can get a job at?

HOLLOWAY. What kind of job you looking for?

STERLING. Any kind. I can do anything.

WOLF. Go up and see Hendricks. He got a construction company.

STERLING. That's who I was working for. He helped me get out the penitentiary. I work for him one week and he laid me off say he ain't had enough business to keep me working. He say he'd call me if he had any work for me.

MEMPHIS. Go on over the steel mill. A big strong boy like you...if you ain't scared of work...they got work over there.

STERLING. That's what Hendricks told me. I went over to J&L Steel and they told me I got to join the union before I could work. I went down to the union and they told me I got to be working before I could join the union. They told me to go back to the steel mill and they'd put me on a waiting list. I went and asked my landlady if I could put her on a waiting list. She told me if I didn't give her twelve dollars by Friday I could wait on the street.

HOLLOWAY. You can go up to Boykins and see if he need anybody. You know Boykins up on Herron what got that junkyard? He always complaining he can't keep nobody. That's probably 'cause he don't pay nothing. But you can go up there and see him.

STERLING. I ain't got nothing to lose. I'll go up there. Thanks. Anybody want to buy a watch? *(doesn't get any response)* I carried it up to the pawnshop...he didn't want it either. It got seventeen jewels. That's what it say right here. I don't know what kind of jewels they are... they don't tell you that part. It's liable to be anything. You open it up it's liable to be diamonds and rubies, I don't know. I started to do that, but I didn't know if I could put it back together. You take something apart you should know how to put it back together. Seventeen jewels! And I can't get five dollars for it. *(to* **WOLF***)* I'll let you have it for three dollars.

WOLF. I can't use it.

STERLING. *(holding the watch out to* **MEMPHIS** *and* **HOLLOWAY***)* Three dollars?

(He doesn't get a response.)

That's all right, I'm gonna keep it. I'm gonna keep it till it stop ticking. Whenever you see me I'm gonna have on this watch.

WOLF. Well, let me get on and make my day. I'll see you all later. Hey, Risa… keep smiling, baby.

(**WOLF** *exits.*)

STERLING. *(looking out the window)* They got so many people lined up across the street I thought it was the surplus food line. I'm gonna go over and get in line with everybody else. Get my luck changed. *(to **HOLLOWAY**)* You believe in luck? I was born with it. I was born with seven cents. My mama swallowed a nickel and two pennies and I come out with the nickel in one hand and the two pennies in the other. They say I was born with· luck but they didn't say what kind. I think it was bad luck. What you think?

(**RISA** *enters from the back.*)

*(to **RISA**)* Say, baby, give me another cup of coffee. *(to **HOLLOWAY**)* You been over there to see Prophet Samuel?

HOLLOWAY. Yeah, I done seen him.

STERLING. I was over there talking to one man he say if you rub his head you get good luck. One man found twenty dollars on the sidewalk on his way out. I'm going over there. Might go through the line twice. Have double luck. That might not even be enough the way things is going. Might have to go through there three times.

HOLLOWAY. These niggers lining up over there to rub Prophet Samuel's head 'cause they think that's gonna make their hand itch and they gonna get some money. They don't know to go see Aunt Ester. Aunt Ester give you more than money. She make you right with yourself. You ain't got to go far. She live at 1839 Wylie. In the back. Go up there and you'll see a red door. Go up there and knock on that.

HAMBONE. *(suddenly)* I want my ham. I want my ham.

HOLLOWAY. Aunt Ester got a power 'cause she got an understanding. Anybody live as long as she has is bound to have an understanding.

HAMBONE. He gonna give me my ham. I want my ham.

STERLING. Somebody got his ham. *(to* **HAMBONE***)* Who got your ham, man? Somebody took your ham?

HOLLOWAY. He talking about Lutz across the street. He painted his fence for him nine...almost ten years ago, and Lutz told him he'd give him a ham. After he painted the fence Lutz told him to take a chicken. He say he wanted his ham. Lutz told him to take a chicken or don't take nothing. So he wait over there every morning till Lutz come to open his store and he tell him he wants his ham. He ain't got it yet.

MEMPHIS. That ain't how it went. Lutz told him if he painted his fence he'd give him a chicken. Told him if he do a good job he'd give him a ham. He think he did a good job and Lutz didn't. That's where he went wrong – letting Lutz decide what to pay him for his work. If you leave it like that, quite naturally he gonna say it ain't worth the higher price.

HAMBONE. He gonna give me my ham. He gonna give me my ham. I want my ham.

MEMPHIS. *(to* **HAMBONE***)* All right! I told you...that's enough of that!

HAMBONE. *(to himself)* He gonna give me my ham. He gonna give me my ham.

HOLLOWAY. All he got to do is go see Aunt Ester. Aunt Ester could straighten him out. Don't care whatever your problem. She can straighten it out.

STERLING. You think she can help me find a job? I wanna open me up a nightclub.

HOLLOWAY. Whatever your problem is. It don't make no difference to Aunt Ester. She can help you with anything.

STERLING. Where she live at? What's that address again?

HOLLOWAY. 1839 Wylie. In the back. Knock on the red door. You can't miss it. Don't care who answer. Just say you come to see Aunt Ester. You ain't got to tell them what you want to see her about. Just say, "I come to see Aunt Ester." You got to pay her, though. She won't take no money herself. She tell you to go down and throw it into the river. Say it'll come to her. She must be telling the truth, 'cause she don't want for nothing. She got some people there to take care of her and they don't want for nothing either.

MEMPHIS. Ask her how old she is while you up there.

HOLLOWAY. She'll tell you. She don't try to hide it. And she don't care if you believe or not. She three hundred and twenty-two years old. She'll tell you.

MEMPHIS. How the hell somebody gonna live to be three hundred and twenty-two years old, nigger? You talk like a fool.

STERLING. They lived that long in the Bible. I ain't surprised to hear that. Do she look like she come out the Bible?

HOLLOWAY. You got to go see what she look like for yourself. I'm just telling you she three hundred and twenty-two years old. Go on up there and see her. I go up to see her every once in a while. Get my soul washed. She don't do nothing but lay her hands on your head. But it's a feeling like you ain't never had before. Then everything in your life get real calm and peaceful.

MEMPHIS. I'd rather believe if I rubbed Prophet Samuel's head I'd get rich. That make more sense to me than to talk about somebody being three hundred and twenty-two years old.

HOLLOWAY. She look like she five hundred. You be surprised when she say she ain't but three hundred and twenty-two. Don't ask me how she lived that long. I don't know. Look like death scared of her. Every time he come around her he just get up and get on away. Ask West about her. He'll tell you. He done went up there to see her. He been waiting to bury her since he saw her. Even told the people there in the house that he'd do it for free.

MEMPHIS. I ain't seen her change nobody's luck. Every nigger I know got bad luck. If it was easy as that...hell, we'd all be rich.

HOLLOWAY. See? There you go talking about being rich.
I ain't talking about that. I ain't said nothing about
getting rich. I'm talking about getting your luck
changed. You go up there with the wrong attitude and
come out with worse luck than you had before. That's
what the problem is now. Aunt Ester don't buy into
that. She don't make people rich. You go up there
talking about you wanna get rich and she won't have
nothing to do with you. She send you to see Prophet
Samuel...and you see how far that'll get you. Most
people don't know Prophet Samuel went to see Aunt
Ester. He wasn't always a prophet. He started out he
was a reverend. Had him a truck, and he'd stand on
the back of that truck...had him a loudspeaker, and
he'd go out and preach the word of the gospel and
sell barbecue on the side. Everybody knew Reverend
Samuel. He even went out where the white folks lived
and tried to preach to them. They seen him with that
truck and thought he come out there to steal their
furniture. Called the police on him. Many a time. He
go on and pay his fifty-dollar fine for preaching without
a permit and go on back out here.

They had him in big trouble one time. He had all his
money going to his church and they arrested him for
income-tax evasion. That's when he went to see Aunt
Ester. He walked in there a reverend and walked out a
prophet. I don't know what she told him. But he went
down to see the mayor. Say if they arrested him they
had to arrest Mellon too. Say God was gonna send a
sign. The next day the stock market fell so fast they had
to close it early. Mellon called the mayor and told him
to drop the charges. The next day the stock market
went right on back up there. Except for Gulf Oil,
which Mellon owned. That went higher than it ever
went before. Mellon was tickled pink. He sent Prophet
Samuel a five-hundred-dollar donation and a brochure
advertising his banking services. Had his picture taken
with him and everything. That's when Prophet Samuel

went big. The police didn't bother him no more. Wouldn't even give him a parking ticket. If he hadn't started walking around in them robes going barefoot and whatnot...ain't no telling how big he would have got. A lot of people didn't like him wearing them robes...baptizing people in the river and all that kinda stuff.

MEMPHIS. That's the damnedest thing I ever heard of.

HOLLOWAY. Don't take my word for it. Go on up there and see for yourself. Go knock on the door. You don't have to be scared.

MEMPHIS. I ain't scared. What I got to be scared of? I just don't believe all that stuff.

HOLLOWAY. Ask West when you see him. Ask anybody that's been up there.

STERLING. You can ask me when I come back. 1839 Wylie? In the back?

HOLLOWAY. Knock on the red door. Just say you come to see Aunt Ester. She'll straighten you out.

STERLING. Say Risa, cook me up some chicken. I'll be back. I wanna eat what you been eating. See if I can get nice and healthy too.

(**STERLING** *exits.*)

MEMPHIS. That boy ain't got good sense.

(*The lights go down on the scene.*)

Scene Two

(The lights come up on the restaurant. **WOLF** *is looking out the window of the door.* **MEMPHIS** *is at the end of the counter.* **RISA** *is in the back. The winning number, 229, is written on the board.)*

WOLF. Here he come now. Lutz coming down the street. Hambone standing there.

(**MEMPHIS** *comes around the corner of the counter and walks to the door and looks out.)*

MEMPHIS. What's Holloway doing?

WOLF. He watching him. He just standing there. He wanna hear what they say. Look at him...look at him. Look at Hambone.

RISA. *(entering from the back)* What you all looking at?

WOLF. We watching Hambone. We want to see what he say to Lutz. Holloway went over there to stand on the corner. Hambone talking to Lutz now.

MEMPHIS. That's the damnedest thing I ever seen. *(walks back around the counter)* Risa, you been here for a half an hour and ain't got the coffee on. What you doing back there?

Get them grits cooked up. I told you put the bread in the refrigerator...keep it fresh.

WOLF. Lutz going in his store. He turned his back to him and opening up his store. Holloway still standing there. *(turning from the window)* Lutz ought to go on and give him a ham.

MEMPHIS. Lutz ain't gonna give him no ham...'cause he don't feel he owe him. I wouldn't give him one either.

WOLF. After all this time it don't make no difference. He ought to go on and give him a ham. What difference do it make? It ain't like he ain't got none. Got a whole store full of hams.

MEMPHIS. *(to* **RISA**) What'd you do with that flour? Ain't even got the oven turned on. How you gonna cook biscuits without turning on the oven? Where the flour? I brought ten pound of flour in here yesterday.

RISA. It's in the back.

MEMPHIS. Here's the sifter. Sift the baking soda and flour together. You ain't used this sifter in a month. And get on up to the bakery and get West his pie before he get over here.

(RISA *exits to the back.*)

WOLF. I hear tell somebody tried to break in West's last night to steal Prophet Samuel's money and jewels. Set off the burglar alarm...woke West up.

(HOLLOWAY *enters.*)

Hey, Holloway, we was watching you. What Hambone say? We seen Lutz when he come down the street. What he say?

HOLLOWAY. He told him he wanted his ham, that's all. Said, "I want my ham." Lutz told him, "Take a chicken," then he went on in his store. That was it. He ain't said nothing back to him. The only words exchanged was, "I want my ham" and "Take a chicken."

MEMPHIS. I would just like to know...after nine-and-a-half years...am I right, Holloway? ...After nine-and-a-half years...every day... I wish my arithmetic was right to tell you how many days that is...nine-and-a-half years... every day...how...in his right mind...do he think Lutz is gonna give him his ham? You answer me that. That's all I want to know.

WOLF. Anybody can see he ain't in his right mind.

HOLLOWAY. I don't know. He might be more in his right mind than you are. He might have more sense than any of us.

WOLF. Would you stand over there every morning for nine-and-a-half years?

HOLLOWAY. I ain't saying that. Naw...hell, no... I wouldn't stand over there for nine-and-a-half years. But maybe I ain't got as much sense as he got.

MEMPHIS. You tell me how that make sense. You tell me what sense that make?

HOLLOWAY. All right. I'll tell you. Now you take me or you. We ain't gonna do that. We gonna go ahead and forget about it. We might take a chicken. Then we gonna go home and cook that chicken. But how it gonna taste? It can't taste good to us. We gonna be eating just to be eating. How we gonna feel good about ourselves? Every time we even look at a chicken we gonna have a bad taste in our mouth. That chicken's gonna call up that taste. It's gonna make you feel ashamed. Even if it be walking around flapping its wings it's gonna remind us of that bad taste. We ain't gonna tell nobody about it. We don't want nobody to know. But you can't erase it. You got to carry it around with you. This fellow here... he say he don't want to carry it around with him. But he ain't willing to forget about it. He trying to put the shame on the other foot. He trying to shame Lutz into giving him his ham. And if Lutz ever break down and give it to him...he gonna have a big thing. He gonna have something he be proud to tell everybody. He gonna tell his grandkids if he have any. That's why I say he might have more sense than me and you. 'Cause he ain't willing to accept whatever the white man throw at him. It be easier. But he say he don't mind getting out of the bed in the morning to go at what's right. I don't believe you and me got that much sense.

MEMPHIS. That's that old backward Southern mentality. When I come up here they had to teach these niggers they didn't have to tip their hat to a white man. They walking around here tipping their hat, jumping off the sidewalk, talking about, "Yessir, Captain," "How do, Major."

WOLF. How long you been up here, Memphis?

MEMPHIS. I been up here since '36. They ran me out of Jackson in '31. I hung around Natchez for three or four years, then I come up here. I was born in Jackson. I used to farm down there. They ran me out in '31.

Killed my mule and everything. One of these days I'm going back and get my land. I still got the deed.

HOLLOWAY. I got an uncle and a bunch of cousins down in Jackson.

MEMPHIS. When I left out of Jackson I said I was gonna buy me a V-8 Ford and drive by Mr. Henry Ford's house and honk the horn. If anybody come to the window I was gonna wave. Then I was going out and buy me a 30.06, come on back to Jackson and drive up to Mr. Stovall's house and honk the horn. Only this time I wasn't waving. Only thing was, it took me thirteen years to get the Ford. Six years later I traded that in on a Cadillac. But I'm going back one of these days. I ain't even got to know the way. All I got to do is find my way down to the train depot. They got two trains running every day. I used to know the schedule. They might have changed it...but if they did, they got it posted up on the board.

RISA. (entering from the back) The oven's on. I'm going to get the pie.

(RISA exits. MEMPHIS watches after her.)

MEMPHIS. A man would be happy to have a woman like that except she done ruined herself. She ain't right with herself...how she gonna be right with you? Anybody take a razor and cut up on herself ain't right. If she cut her legs she might cut your throat. That's the way I see it. Other than that, any man be glad to lay up next to that every night. Something ain't right with a woman don't want no man. That ain't natural. If she say she like women that be another thing. It ain't natural, but that be something else. But somebody that's all confused about herself and don't want nobody... I can't figure out where to put her.

HOLLOWAY. That's what the problem is...you trying to figure out where to put her. I know Risa. She one of them gals that matured quick. And every man that seen her since she was twelve years old think she ought to go lay up with them somewhere. She don't want that. She figure if she made her legs ugly that would force everybody to look at her and see what kind of personality she is.

MEMPHIS. She a mixed-up personality. Anybody can see that. That plain to see. Who want a woman after she done that to herself? I don't want her. I don't know what she might do to me.

HOLLOWAY. They had her down there at Western Psych. They couldn't find nothing wrong with her. They tried every kind of counselor they could think of.

WOLF. She don't need no counselor. Ain't nothing wrong with Risa. All she need is a good man. Trust me, I know Risa.

MEMPHIS. You don't know her like you want to know her. Don't nobody know her.

WOLF. I know Risa better than people think I do. That's what I'm trying to say. I know all she need is a man. Somebody to make her feel like a woman. She ain't had that in six years that I know of. Common sense say after six years she need a man. I see where that Sterling be eyeing her. He be after her. But he don't know Risa. He don't know her like I know her. Maybe he a better man than me. I don't know. But if I had to say, I don't think so. You want anything, Memphis?

MEMPHIS. Give me a dollar on four twenty-one.

WOLF. Holloway?

HOLLOWAY. I'm gonna wait till I get me a good dream. I can't dream about nothing.

WOLF. I'll catch you all later.

(WOLF *exits.*)

MEMPHIS. Hey Holloway you know what I just found out? You know who that boy is…that Sterling boy? I was talking to Hendricks… That's the boy robbed that bank and was out spending the money ten minutes later. You remember that? Hendricks give him a job to help him get out and the boy worked one week and quit. See,

Hendricks don't know…he don't know like I know. He trying to help him, but that boy don't wanna work.

HOLLOWAY. He say Hendricks laid him off. But I can't blame him if he did quit. Who wanna haul bricks on a construction site for a dollar and a quarter an hour? That ain't gonna help him. What's he gonna do with ten dollars a day?

MEMPHIS. That be ten more than he got now. His grandaddy used to work for three dollars a day. He doing good!

HOLLOWAY. I ain't talking about that. Hell, his great-grandaddy used to work for nothing, for all that matter. I'm talking about he can make two or three hundred dollars a day gambling…if he get lucky. If he don't, somebody else will get it. That's all you got around here is niggers with somebody else's money in their pocket. And they don't do nothing but trade it off on each other. I got it today and you got it tomorrow. Until sooner or later as sure as the sun shine…somebody gonna take it and give it to the white man. The money go from you to me to you and then – bingo – it's gone. From him to you to me, then – bingo – it's gone. You give it to the white man. Pay your rent, pay your telephone, buy your groceries, see the doctor – bingo – it's gone. Just circulate it around till it find that hole, then – bingo. Like trying to haul sand in a bucket with a hole in it. Time you get where you going the bucket empty. That's why that ten dollars a day ain't gonna do him no good. A nigger with five hundred dollars in his pocket around here is a big man. But you go out there where they at…you go out to Squirrel Hill, they walking around there with five thousand dollars in their pocket trying to figure out how to make it into five hundred thousand.

MEMPHIS. Ain't nothing wrong in saving your money and do like they do. These niggers just don't want to work. That boy don't want to work. He lazy.

HOLLOWAY. People kill me talking about niggers is lazy.
Niggers is the most hardworking people in the world.
Worked three hundred years for free. And didn't take
no lunch hour. Now all of a sudden niggers is lazy.
Don't know how to work. All of a sudden when they
got to pay niggers, ain't no work for him to do. If it
wasn't for you the white man would be poor. Every little
bit he got he got standing on top of you. That's why
he could reach so high. He give you three dollars a
day for six months and he got him a railroad for the
next hundred years. All you got is six months' worth of
three dollars a day.

(RISA *enters carrying a pie box.*)

Now you can't even get that. Ain't no money in niggers
working. Look out there on the street. If there was some
money in it...if the white man could figure out a way to
make some money by putting niggers to work...we'd all
be working. He ain't building no more railroads. He got
them. He ain't building no more highways. Somebody
done already stuck the telephone poles in the ground.
That's been done already. The white man ain't stacking
no more niggers. You know what I'm talking about,
stacking niggers, don't you? Well, here's how that go.
If you ain't got nothing...you can go out here and get
you a nigger. Then you got something, see. You got
one nigger. If that one nigger get out there and plant
something...get something out the ground...even if it
ain't nothing but a bushel of potatoes...then you got
one nigger and one bushel of potatoes. Then you take
that bushel of potatoes and go get you another nigger.
Then you got two niggers. Put them to work and you got
two niggers and two bushels of potatoes. See, now you
can go buy two more niggers. That's how you stack a
nigger on top of a nigger. White folks got to stacking...
and I'm talking about they stacked up some niggers!
Stacked up close to fifty million niggers. If you stacked
them on top of one another they make six or seven

circles around the moon. It's lucky the boat didn't sink with all them niggers they had stacked up there. It take them two extra months to get here 'cause it ride so low in the water. They couldn't find you enough work back then. Now that they got to pay you they can't find you none. If this was different time wouldn't be nobody out there on the street. They'd all be in the cotton fields.

MEMPHIS. I still say that boy don't want to work.

(WEST *enters. He is a widower in his early sixties. He is dressed all in black except for a white shirt. He wears a pair of black gloves. Since his wife's death he has allowed his love of money to overshadow the other possibilities of life.*)

HOLLOWAY. Hey, West.

WEST. Hey, Risa.

RISA. How you doing, Mr. West?

(*She puts his coffee in front of him and goes to get the pie.*)

WEST. Let me get a little bit of sugar here, Risa.

MEMPHIS. I see they lined up out there.

WEST. Yeah, I finally got him laid out like they wanted and the people over there trying to rub his head. I got it roped off, but they duck right under the rope talking about they didn't see it.

MEMPHIS. I ain't been over there yet, but Holloway say they got all kind of jewels and hundred-dollar bills in the casket with him.

WEST. I don't know how that got started. The man ain't got nothing but a couple of rings, that gold cross he wear, and two hundred-dollar bills. Got one in his breast pocket and one wrapped around his finger...tucked and glued in his hand.

MEMPHIS. You ain't glued the man's money in his hand.

WEST. Yeah, I did. I done learned in this business. I can't tell you how many rings and watches and whatnot have disappeared.

MEMPHIS. I know you ain't gonna put that money in the ground.

WEST. I'll bury anything with anybody. You be surprised what people want in the casket with them. I done buried people with Bibles, canes, crutches, guitars, radios, baby dolls… One lady brought some tomatoes from her sister's garden. She didn't just want me to put them in there. She wanted to tell me where to put them. That wouldn't have been so bad, but she kept changing her mind. People's something. They don't understand about dead folks. Dead folks don't know nothing. They don't know them tomatoes is in there with them. But the family know. That's who it's important to. It took me a while to figure that out… But I don't mind putting anything in there with anybody as long as the casket close.

MEMPHIS. Is you gonna put that money in the ground? That's what I wanna know.

WEST. Most times the family come and get the money before you close the casket. Take off their rings and everything else. I hate to even lay people out with jewelry…'cause the family come and remind you every day that it ain't supposed to go in the ground.

MEMPHIS. Holloway say they was over there taking up a collection. Say they was charging the people to see him.

WEST. I put a stop to that. I don't allow that kind of thing over there. I stopped them from doing that. What they say to you downtown there?

MEMPHIS. I ain't went yet. I got to go down there tomorrow. I'm going down there and see what they offer me for it. I ain't taking a penny less than twenty-five thousand dollars.

WEST. They ain't gonna give you no twenty-five thousand dollars for this building. It ain't worth that. They look up what you paid for it and double that. That's one hundred percent profit. They figure anybody be satisfied with that. It's hard to argue against that. The lawyer can't even argue against that. They ain't gonna give you but ten…eleven thousand. Twelve at the most.

MEMPHIS. I ain't taking a penny less than twenty-five thousand.

WEST. They ain't gonna give you no twenty-five thousand dollars on something they gonna tear down! I don't know how niggers think sometimes. Now, I told you I'd give you fifteen thousand dollars for it. Cash money. We can go down to the bank right now. Fifteen thousand dollars. Draw it right out in cash. You can get it any way you want. Hundreds. Twenties.

MEMPHIS. Naw. Naw. I ain't taking a penny less than twenty-five thousand dollars.

WEST. You watch and see what I'm telling you. They gonna double what you paid for it. They ain't gonna give you no ten thousand dollars on top of that.

MEMPHIS. Then they ain't getting my building. I figure that twenty-five thousand is cheap. They forcing me to move out…close up my business…well, I figure they ought to pay something for that. I don't care what the building is worth or how much I bought it for.

WEST. They got the right of eminent domain. They don't care what you think. They can go anywhere in the city and take any piece of property they want. The city council done voted to take over these whole twelve blocks. They getting five this year and seven next year. They ain't gonna let you stand in their way. Talk to Philmore down the street. He sold me his place. He know the city wasn't gonna give him what it's worth.

MEMPHIS. Give me twenty-five thousand dollars and you can have it. Put it with your other property and go down there and get fifty for it.

WEST. I told you I'd give you fifteen. It ain't worth no twenty-five. To me or nobody else.

MEMPHIS. I ain't taking a penny less than twenty-five thousand dollars.

WEST. All right. You gonna be surprised. Don't say I didn't warn you. Let me know if you change your mind. We can go right on down to the bank any time you want.

(WEST *exits.*)

MEMPHIS. You hear that, Holloway? The man own so much property around here the city gonna go broke trying to pay him for it and he trying to hustle me. Hell, if he offer me fifteen for it I know it's worth twenty-five. Might be able to get thirty.

(STERLING *enters. He has a handful of flyers.*)

STERLING. How you all doing? Hey, Risa, let me get a cup of coffee.

HOLLOWAY. Did you go up there to see Aunt Ester?

STERLING. I went up there. Got a red door just like you say. I knocked on the door. I must have knocked on it about five minutes. I was getting ready to leave when a man opened the door. Big man. Must have been over seven feet tall. I told him I wanted to see Aunt Ester and he told me she was sick.

HOLLOWAY. She get sick sometime. As you can imagine somebody three hundred and twenty-two years old is bound to get sick once in a while. But she ain't gonna die, I guarantee you that! You go on back up there next week.

MEMPHIS. Ain't nobody up there. I take that back…there might be somebody up there but she ain't no three hundred years old.

HOLLOWAY. Three hundred and twenty-two. If you gonna tell it tell it right. Three hundred and twenty-two.

(STERLING *hands a flyer to* MEMPHIS *and* HOLLOWAY.)

STERLING. You all wanna go to this rally. They having a rally to celebrate Malcolm X's birthday. It's right down there at the Savoy Ballroom.

(They read the flyers. **STERLING** *hands one to* **RISA**.*)*

Here you go, Risa.

MEMPHIS. Malcolm X is dead. Malcolm ain't having no more birthdays. Dead men don't have birthdays. I'd rather celebrate your birthday. I'll buy the cake, a case of liquor, and we can have a party. I ain't going to no party for no dead man.

HOLLOWAY. I remember when Malcolm didn't have but twelve followers. I remember when he come out to the mosque there. I went out and saw him. He didn't have but twelve followers.

STERLING. Why wasn't you number thirteen?

MEMPHIS. Where he gonna follow him to? The only place he was going was to the graveyard. Anybody could see that.

HOLLOWAY. I didn't follow him 'cause I know where to find Aunt Ester. If she hadn't been there I don't know what I would have done.

STERLING. I would have followed him. He the only one who told the truth. That's why they killed him.

MEMPHIS. Niggers killed Malcolm. Niggers killed Malcolm. When you want to talk about Malcolm, remember that first. Niggers killed Malcolm...and now they want to celebrate his birthday.

HOLLOWAY. Malcolm got too big. People call him a saint. That's what the problem was. He got too big, and when you get that big ain't nothing else you could do. They killed all the saints. Saint Peter. Saint Paul. They killed them all. When you get to be a saint there ain't nothing else you can do but die. The people wouldn't have it any other way.

MEMPHIS. You right about that. They killed Martin. If they did that to him you can imagine what they do to me or you. If they kill the sheep you know what they do to the wolf.

STERLING. That's why they having the rally. They rallying for black power. Stop them from killing the sheep.

MEMPHIS. That's what half the problem is...these Black Power niggers. They got people confused. They don't know what they doing themselves. These niggers talking about freedom, justice and equality and don't know what it mean. You born free. It's up to you to maintain it. You born with dignity and everything else. These niggers talking about freedom, but what you gonna do with it? Freedom is heavy. You got to put your shoulder to freedom. Put your shoulder to it and hope your back hold up. And if you around here looking for justice, you got a long wait. Ain't no justice. That's why they got that statue of her and got her blindfolded. Common sense would tell you if anybody need to see she do. There ain't no justice. Jesus Christ didn't get justice. What makes you think you gonna get it? That's just the nature of the world. These niggers talking about they want freedom, justice and equality. Equal to what? Hell, I might be a better man than you. What I look like going around here talking about I want to be equal to you? I don't know how these niggers think sometimes. Talking about black power with their hands and their pockets empty. You can't do nothing without a gun. Not in this day and time. That's the only kind of power the white man understand. They think they gonna talk their way up on it. In order to talk your way you got to have something under the table. These niggers don't understand that. If I tell you to get out my yard and leave my apples alone, I can't talk you out. You sit up in the tree and laugh at me. But if you know I might come out with a shotgun...that be something different. You'd have to think twice about whether you wanted some apples. These niggers around here talking about they black and beautiful. Sound like they trying to convince themselves. You got to think you ugly to run around shouting you beautiful. You don't hear me say that. Hell, I know I look nice. Got good manners and everything.

STERLING. Well, it say, "Come one, come all." You supposed to be there when it say that. But that's all right – if you don't go, it ain't gonna stop the show.

(HAMBONE *enters.*)

HAMBONE. He gonna give me my ham. He gonna give me my ham.

MEMPHIS. Naw. Naw. Take that on out of here. Risa, don't give him nothing. Go on, take that somewhere else.

HAMBONE. He gonna give me my ham. He gonna give me my ham.

MEMPHIS. I don't wanna hear that today. Go on out of here with that.

RISA. Here's your coffee, Hambone.

MEMPHIS. I told you not to give him nothing.

RISA. He ain't bothering nobody.

MEMPHIS. Let him take that somewhere else.

(MEMPHIS *comes around the counter, takes the coffee from* HAMBONE, *and throws it out.*)

RISA. He ain't bothering nobody, Memphis. He just come in to get his coffee.

HAMBONE. *(to* MEMPHIS*)* He gonna give me my ham.

MEMPHIS. *(pushing* HAMBONE *toward the door)* Go on over there and get it.

HAMBONE. I want my ham!

MEMPHIS. *(at the door)* There he is. Go on over there.

(HAMBONE *exits.*)

Come in here running off at the mouth. I'm tired of hearing that.

RISA. He don't bother nobody.

MEMPHIS. He bother me. Let him go on over there and get his ham. It ain't like Lutz hiding from him. That man crazy. He let Lutz drive him crazy. Well, go on over there with Lutz and tell *him*. Don't tell me. Man been around here ten years talking the same thing. I'm tired of hearing it.

> (**MEMPHIS** *slams the restaurant door closed. The lights go down on the scene.*)

Scene III

(The lights come up on the restaurant. **STERLING**
*sits at the counter eating a bowl of beans. The
number is 460.* **RISA** *is in the back.)*

STERLING. Say, Risa, what you put in these beans? You must
have stuck your finger in there or something. Give me
another bowl. Give me a couple of them muffins too.

*(***RISA** *enters from the back. She brings* **STERLING**
a bowl of beans.)

I went up to see Boykins about a job. He say he don't
need nobody. He told me to go over to the steel mill.
He don't know they got a waiting list.

RISA. Everybody got a waiting list.

STERLING. I saw Hambone. I was trying to talk to him. We
got us a thing going.

RISA. Most people don't understand Hambone. That's
'cause they don't take the time. Most people think
he can't understand nothing. But he understand
everything what's going on around him. Most of the
time he understand better than they do.

STERLING. I seen Holloway a little while ago. He say he
was going downtown to see about his social security. I
didn't know he was that old. He say he was going down
there and register.

RISA. He used to paint houses. Sometime he still do that.
Going up on people's roofs. I told him you'd never
catch me going up there.

STERLING. I wouldn't go up lessen it was flat on top. Then
I wouldn't mind none. Where Memphis?

RISA. He gone downtown to take care of his business. They
gonna tear the building down.

STERLING. That don't surprise me. Ain't nothing hardly
around here no more no way. They done tore the
orphanage down. I was born an orphan. My mama gave
me away to Mrs. Johnson. She died and they put me in

an orphanage. Down there at Toner Institute. I been on my own since I was eighteen. That's twelve years now. I made it pretty good so far. Except when I was in the penitentiary.

RISA. What you go to jail for?

STERLING. I robbed a bank. I was tired of waking up every day with no money. I figure a man supposed to have money sometime. Everybody else seem like they got it. Seem like I'm the only one ain't got no money. I figure I'd get my money where Mellon get his from. That was after Mr. Lewis at the orphanage died. I never would want him to know I would do something like that. After he died I got kinda desperate. I just kept getting deeper and deeper in a hole… Wolf say you put them scars on your legs yourself. Wasn't you scared you was gonna bleed to death?

RISA. They didn't bleed that much.

STERLING. I be scared to do something like that. We had one boy down at the Toner Institute…name of Eddie Langston… I never will forget that. He cut his wrists and bled to death. We was about thirteen. I tried to wake him up in the morning and the whole bed was filled with blood. That stopped me from doing something like that. You wanna go to this rally with me? They having this rally for Malcolm X. You ought to come and go with me. It right down there at the Savoy Ballroom. They might have some dancing. You like to dance?

RISA. If it be with the right person.

STERLING. I can't dance. I ain't never danced. I guess I could slow-dance. Seem like anybody can do that. That ain't but so much grinding. I can't fast-dance though. It seems kinda stupid to be moving around like that. Like you should know better than to make yourself look silly.

RISA. It ain't silly. You can't dance for real?

STERLING. I asked this girl one time and she said no. I ain't never asked nobody else. I started to one time. Something told me not to. It was down at the Workmen's Club. I went in there and seen this woman. She was dancing with some other guys. She was laughing and having her a good time. I started to ask her to dance and changed my mind. Then I just forgot about dancing for good.

RISA. You just didn't ask the right person.

STERLING. You ought to hang that announcement up there. Somebody might wanna go. It say, "Come one, come all." You ought to come and go with me.

RISA. I don't want to go down there with all them people. I stay away from all that kind of stuff. You never see me hanging around a bunch of people.

STERLING. People don't pay you half as much mind as you think they do. That just be in your head. Most people so busy trying to live their own lives they ain't got time to pay attention to nobody else. I found that out. I used to think everybody cared what I did. I robbed that bank and thought people would be mad at me. Half of them didn't even know I was gone. Five years and ain't nobody missed me. They didn't even think about me till they saw me again. You can go down there with me and won't nobody even notice.

RISA. I don't care if they notice or not. I don't want to go down there with them niggers. There might be a riot or something.

STERLING. If a fight break out, you just get behind me. I won't let nobody hurt you. Not when you with me. I don't care if he was King Kong or Mighty Joe Young. He got to come through me first. Mrs. Johnson taught me that. Told me not to let nobody hurt my sister. Say she'd rather see me hurt than her hurt. That made me kinda important. Made me feel strong. Like when I robbed the bank. That made me feel strong too. Like I had everything under control. I did until they arrested me.

RISA. I still ain't going down there.

STERLING. I can't find no job, I got to keep trying to hit the numbers. You play numbers?

RISA. I don't throw my money away like that.

STERLING. I know a lot of people play numbers. If you lucky you can do all right. I been trying to hit since I got out. I dreamt about dogs and looked it up in the dream book. That didn't work. I found a quarter on the fourth step of my house and played four twenty-five. That didn't work. Now I'm counting cars. I count all the Buicks I see and play that with all the Cadillacs and Fords I see. If I had a telephone number I'd play that.

RISA. I don't know why people throw their money away. That twenty-five cents you found is twenty-five cents you could have had. You could have played the jukebox or something.

STERLING. I'm trying to get twenty-five hundred dollars. I wouldn't mind taking a chance on that if I had me a good number.

RISA. Play seven eighty-one.

STERLING. How you come up with that?

RISA. I got seven scars on one leg and eight on the other.

STERLING. Where you get the one from?

RISA. That's my business.

STERLING. One what?

RISA. Go on, Sterling, I ain't playing with you.

STERLING. What? I just say, "Where you get the one from?" You getting all embarrassed. What you getting embarrassed about? I ought to play seven eighty-two. We can put one and one together.

RISA. Go on, Sterling. You asked me for a number and I give you one now. If you want to play it go on and play it.

STERLING. I'm gonna put five dollars on that number seven eighty-one. Wait – let me see how much money I got. (*looks in his pocket*) I ain't got nothing right now, but as soon as I get me some money I'm gonna play that seven eighty-one. If it come out we gonna get married.

(**HOLLOWAY** *enters.*)

Hey, Holloway.

HOLLOWAY. Hey, Sterling. How you doing, Risa?

STERLING. Hey, Holloway, you talking about that fence that run in back of Lutz's Meat Market where he put his garbage, back of that alley there, across from that billboard above Eddie's Restaurant? Is that the fence Hambone painted?

HOLLOWAY. Yeah, that's it.

STERLING. That fence run all up the side and all the way around the back there. He ought to have give him two hams. I wouldn't paint that fence for no ham. He'd have to give me a case of chickens or one of them half-cows he got hanging over there. He'd have to give me something like that. That fence run all the way back around there.

HOLLOWAY. Used to have another part closer to the front, but Lutz tore that down.

STERLING. I looked at it. He did a good job. Some of the paint done chipped off but you can tell he did a good job. I started to go over there and get his ham for him. But then he wouldn't have nothing to do in the morning. I didn't want to take that away from him. He have more cause to get up out of the bed in the morning than I do. I consider him lucky. I get up 'cause I wake up and can't think of nothing else to do. Get up and see what's out here. Only it be the same thing as yesterday. I guess it be that for him, too. Only Lutz just might shock him to death one day and say, "Here, take your ham!" Best thing that might happen to me is I get a woman and an extra twenty dollars from somewhere. The jukebox still broke?

RISA. Yeah. They supposed to fix it. It ain't gonna do nothing but break again if they do fix it.

STERLING. I don't know why I want to play it. That's just like paying a quarter to hear yourself sing. You ought to get a radio or something. That's free.

HOLLOWAY. Let me get some sugar, Risa.

STERLING. How come you don't give nobody no sugar? You make them ask for it.

RISA. I give it to them. All they got to do is ask. West ask for sugar and then half the time don't use it. You watch him. First thing he do is ask for sugar and then it look like he change his mind.

STERLING. West got a sweet tooth. I'm surprised he don't use it. As much pie as he eat.

(WOLF *enters.*)

WOLF. How's everybody in here? Risa, here go some stockings. And put this cologne back over there for Memphis. He like that English Leather cologne.

RISA. What size is they?

WOLF. They your size. I wouldn't be giving them to you otherwise.

RISA. How much I owe you?

WOLF. You don't owe me nothing. If I come up with one of them fur coats we can sit down and talk. We can do some real nice negotiating.

RISA. I don't want no fur coat.

WOLF. You don't want none till you see it. After you put one of them on and see what it feel like…then you want one.

STERLING. Hey Wolf…loan me two dollars. I wanna play a number. Me and Risa got something going. Luck might be trying to get in my door today. I need me some money to buy Risa a present.

WOLF. I ain't got it, Sterling.

STERLING. I'm gonna hit the numbers and buy Risa a present, then I'm gonna get me one of them Buick Electra deuce and a quarter.

HOLLOWAY. You need to be trying to find you a job.

STERLING. I been trying to get one. Ain't nobody got none. I wish I could get one of them white folks' job making eight or nine thousand dollars a year.

HOLLOWAY. You ain't got none of them white folks' education...how you gonna get one of their jobs?

STERLING. Hey, I can do anything. I told the judge I could do his job. I got enough sense to sit up there and tell right from wrong. I can tell when somebody getting railroaded...when the lawyer is talking too much. I got sense enough to know when it's lunchtime and how to say "Recess." I can do anything the white man can do. If the truth be told...most things I can do better.

HOLLOWAY. I see where you gonna end up back down there.

STERLING. Not in this life. All I do is try to live in the world, but the world done gone crazy. I'm sorry I was ever born into it. This woman told me one time, "Sterling, I wanna have your baby." I told her if we have a baby he might live to be seventy-five years old. Just think how much hell he gonna catch. I wouldn't do that to nobody. She told me I was crazy. Hell, maybe she was right. But nobody will ever come to me and say, "You responsible for this. You brought me into this crazy world."

WOLF. That's why I don't have no kids. I said the same thing.

STERLING. Hey Wolf...tell him...what kind of world is this?

HOLLOWAY. You sit around talking about you want this... you want the other...you want a job...you want a car. What you don't know is everybody that want one got one. You talking about you want one and ain't doing nothing to get none. The people that have them is the people that wanted them. You don't do nothing but sit around and talk about what you ain't got. The more you sit around and talk about what you ain't got the more you have to talk about. Wait two or three years and see what you have to talk about then.

STERLING. I know what I'm doing. I'm gonna get me two or three Cadillacs and everything that go with them. If I can't find no job I might have to find me a gun. Hey Wolf, you know anybody got a gun they want to sell?

WOLF. What you looking for?

STERLING. Something that shoot straight. I don't care what it is. I don't want no twenty-two. A thirty-eight too big and heavy. Everybody can see it's bulging out under your coat. I'll take me a snub-nosed thirty-two if I can get one. I don't want no silver gun that shine in the dark. I'll take a black one. Other than that I don't care what it is.

WOLF. Tony Jackson got an Army forty-five he trying to sell.

STERLING. I don't want no forty-five. He probably got the same one I had. You liable to end up shooting yourself with that. I was shooting at some birds one time and couldn't even hit the tree.

WOLF. I'll ask around. Let me get some sugar, Risa.

HOLLOWAY. I see where you want to go back down the penitentiary. I thought you was trying to stay out.

STERLING. You subject to end up there anyway. You don't have to do nothing to go to jail.

WOLF. You right about that. I know. You can walk down there…just walk down the street and ask people…every nigger you see done been to jail one time or another. The white man don't feel right unless he got a record on these niggers. Walk on down there… I'll give you a dollar for every nigger you find that ain't been to jail. Ain't that right, Sterling. I been to jail. Stayed down there three months. Tried to make bond and couldn't do it. They kept me down there in the county jail for three months. Ain't done nothing but walk down the street. I was walking down Centre Avenue…police was chasing somebody and wasn't looking where he was going, and I wasn't looking where I was going either… he ran into me so hard it knocked us both down. I started to get up and there was two, three policemen with their guns pointed at my head. Told me not to move. They arrested me for obstructing justice. Kept me down there for three months before the judge had a chance to throw it out. But I learned a lot from that. I learned to watch where I was going at all times. 'Cause you always under attack.

STERLING. That's why I said if I was going I was going for something. ·

(HAMBONE *enters.*)

Hey, my man. How you doing, Hambone?

HAMBONE. He gonna give me my ham. He gonna give me my ham.

STERLING. Risa, give him something to eat.

RISA. You hungry Hambone? You want a bowl of beans?

HAMBONE. He gonna give me my ham. He gonna give me my ham.

WOLF. Hey Holloway you know Bubba Boy don't you? Him and his woman?

HOLLOWAY. Yeah…be together all the time. When you see him you see her.

WOLF. I just found out she died. She overdosed last night. West just went down to pick up her body. She dead and he in jail. He went down to Surrey's to get her a dress to be buried in. You know them dresses down there cost two, three hundred dollars. He went down there like a fool and was walking out the door with the dress… they arrested him. He can't even go to her funeral. The people taking up a collection to see if they can get him out on bond. You wanna give anything?

HOLLOWAY. Here go a dollar.

STERLING. Holloway…loan me two dollars.

HOLLOWAY. I ain't got no two dollars. If you had a job you'd have two dollars.

RISA. Holloway ain't got no money… Here.

(RISA *hands* STERLING *two dollars.* STERLING *hands them to* WOLF.)

STERLING. That's for me and Hambone.

HOLLOWAY. How much is his bail?

WOLF. They got him on a two-thousand-dollar bond. I got to get two hundred dollars.

STERLING. Go ask West. He got all that money.

WOLF. West ain't gonna give a dime.

STERLING. Whoever hit the numbers ought to put in ten or twenty.

WOLF. That's what I say but it don't always work like that. Thanks, I'll see you all later.

HOLLOWAY. Let me get a dime on that nine sixty-eight before you go. I dreamt about snakes.

> (**WOLF** *writes the slip.*)

I don't know what Bubba Boy's gonna do now. I ain't never seen him without her. You see him you see her. It's been like that for fifteen years. I used to look at them and say that's how deep love get. I don't know what he gonna do now.

WOLF. I don't know either. But we gonna try and get him out of jail.

> (**WOLF** *exits.* **STERLING** *moves over to the stool next to* **HAMBONE**. **RISA** *gives* **HAMBONE** *a bowl of beans.*)

STERLING. Hey Hambone. How you doing?

HAMBONE. He gonna give me my ham.

STERLING. You want your ham?

RISA. Sterling, don't be playing with him like that.

STERLING. I ain't playing with him. Me and Hambone got us a thing going. Ain't we, Hambone?

HAMBONE. He gonna give me my ham.

STERLING. I'm trying to build up his confidence in me. Ain't that right, Hambone? *(to* **RISA***)* You don't know nothing about this. We talking man to man.
Okay, Hambone, check this out. Now…you ready? First I say it…and then you say it. You ready?

(STERLING lines up in front of HAMBONE.)

Now listen. Take your time. Don't worry about getting it wrong. Okay. *(pronouncing each word carefully)* Black – is – beautiful. See? Come on now. Black…

HAMBONE. Black…

STERLING. Is…

HAMBONE. Is…

STERLING. Beautiful.

HAMBONE. Beautiful.

STERLING. Yeah, see – you got it. Black is beautiful.

HAMBONE. Black is beautiful.

(HAMBONE grins at his accomplishment.)

STERLING. I want you to remember that now…for the next time I see you. Then I'll teach you something else. Okay?

HAMBONE. He gonna give me my ham. He gonna give me my ham.

(MEMPHIS enters.)

MEMPHIS. These white folks crazy. Tell me my deed say they can give me anything they want for my building. Say it got a clause. I told them I don't care nothing about no clause. What kind of sense that make if they can give me what they want?

HOLLOWAY. How much they offer you?

MEMPHIS. Fifteen thousand dollars! I raised all kind of hell. The judge looked at me like I was crazy. I told them I got a clause too. They ain't the only one got a clause. My clause say they got to give me what I want for it. It's my building. If they wanna buy it they got to meet my price. That's just common sense. I raised so much hell the judge postponed it…told me talk to my lawyer. The lawyer looked at the deed and told me that they was right. I told him, "I don't need you no more." Fired him on the spot. He supposed to be on my side. They left it like that till I could get me another lawyer.

HOLLOWAY. Who was your lawyer?

MEMPHIS. Chauncey Ward. Supposed to be a big nigger down there. Chauncey Ward III. His daddy was a judge. You remember Chauncey Ward. The first black judge they had down there. He was death on niggers. Give one fellow five hundred years.

HOLLOWAY. I know Chauncey Ward.

MEMPHIS. This his son. Ain't even looked at the paper good...talking about they right. I don't care what the paper say he supposed to fix it so they meet my price. I left out of there and called me one of them white lawyers, which is what I should have done in the first place. Fellow named Joseph Bartoromo.

STERLING. You got insurance? If you got insurance you could burn it down.

MEMPHIS. Nigger, is you crazy! Insurance cost five times what the building is worth. That's why I keep me some good tenants upstairs. I don't put none of them fools up there that's liable to get drunk and burn down the place. When Mr. Collins died I let it set empty three months till I got somebody up there that was responsible. Look back in the kitchen...ask Risa... I got four or five fire extinguishers back there...and you talking about burning down the place. That's the one thing I am scared of. If it burn down I don't get nothing. I don't even get the fifteen thousand. See, they don't know. The half ain't never been told. I'm ready to walk through fire. I don't bother nobody. The last person I bothered is dead. My mama died in '54. I said then I wasn't going for no more draws. They don't know I feel just like I did when my mama died. She got old and gray and sat by the window till she died. She must have done that 'cause she ain't had nothing else to do. I was gone. My brother was gone. Sister gone. Everybody gone. My daddy was gone. She sat there till she died. I was staying down on Logan Street. Got the letter one day and telegram the next. They usually fall on top of one another...but not that close. I got the letter say "If you wanna see your mother you better come home." Before I could get out the door the telegram came saying, "It's too late...your mother gone." I was trying to borrow some money. Called the train station and found out the schedule and I'm trying to borrow some money. I can't go down there broke. I don't know how long I got to be there. I ain't even got the train fare. I got twelve dollars and sixty-three cents. I got the telegram and sat down and cried like a baby. I could beat any newborn baby in the world crying. I cried till the tears all run down in my ears. Got up and went out the door and everything looked different. Everything had changed. I felt like I had been cut loose. All them years something had a hold of me and I didn't know it. I didn't find out till it cut me loose. I walked out the door and everything had different colors to it. I felt great. I didn't owe nobody nothing. The last person I owed anything to was gone. I borrowed fifty dollars from West and went on down to her funeral. I come back and said, "Everybody better get out my way." You couldn't hold me down. It look like then I had somewhere to go fast. I didn't know where, but I damn sure was going there. That's the way I feel now. They don't know I got a clause of my own. I'll get up off the canvas if I have to. They can carry me out feet first...but my clause say...they got to meet my price!

(The lights go down on the scene.)

ACT TWO

Scene I

*(The lights come up on the restaurant. **RISA** sits on one of the stools. The flyer about the rally is taped to the wall behind the counter. **STERLING** enters with a handful of flowers and a five-gallon gas can. He is dressed in different clothes. He wears a cap instead of a hat.)*

STERLING. Hey Risa. Here.

RISA. What's that?

STERLING. What they look like? Them some flowers. I got them for you.

RISA. Sterling, where you get these flowers from?

STERLING. What you worried about where I got them from? God made them. You don't ask him where he got them from. I got them, that's all that counts.

RISA. Sterling, where you get these flowers from?

STERLING. I got them from across the street. I wasn't gonna buy them. I think that's silly to buy flowers. White folks do that. If I want to buy you something I buy you earrings or something. But I got them. And I got them for you. I saw them and I said, "I'm gonna take these to Risa. She a woman. Woman supposed to like nice things. Flowers and lace and all that kind of stuff." You better look at those flowers and see where they got your name on them. That's all you got to know.

RISA. I don't want no flowers you stole from a dead man.

STERLING. He don't mind. The man got so many flowers West don't know where to put them. West had to postpone his funeral and the flowers sitting over there dying. If I was gonna steal the man's flowers I'd pull a truck up there at night and go on and take the whole load. I picked them four or five 'cause I was thinking of you and I looked and seen where they had your name on it. Now you talking about you don't want them. Hell, a flower's a flower. They gonna be dead in a minute if you don't put them in some water. They gonna be dead in two or three days even if you do. Go on and put them in a glass and enjoy them. Prophet Samuel can't smell them. He don't even know they there. People throwing all that money away buying flowers.

(**RISA** *puts the flowers in a glass.*)

RISA. West gonna come over here and see these flowers. I'm gonna tell him where I got them from.

STERLING. I'll tell him myself. West don't care. He ain't gonna do nothing but take them out there and throw them in the ground.

(**HOLLOWAY** *enters.*)

Hey Holloway, you think Aunt Ester be well yet?

HOLLOWAY. You can go back up there. 1839 Wylie. In the back. Knock on the red door.

STERLING. I got something I wanna ask her about Risa.

RISA. You ain't got nothing to ask her about me.

STERLING. I wanna find out something. I asked God to send me an angel. He said he couldn't do that but he'd send me a teasing brown. I wanna find out if you her. If you is, then...look out, woman! We gonna make all kinds of babies.

(**RISA** *sees the gas can.*)

RISA. Sterling, what's that? Where you get that from?

STERLING. I found it in back of the alley down there off of Centre. In back of that drugstore. It was just sitting there...wasn't nobody around...so I picked it up. It got five gallon of gas in it.

RISA. You done went and stole somebody's gas.

STERLING. I told you I found it, woman.

HOLLOWAY. You ought to put them flowers in a bigger glass. Put a little salt in the glass. They last longer then. That's what my grandmother used to do.

(HAMBONE *enters.*)

STERLING. There he is! Hey, Hambone. Black is beautiful!

(HAMBONE *looks at him for a moment, confused.*)

HAMBONE. I want my ham.

STERLING. You stick with me...you gonna get your ham. Okay? Me and you. Brothers. *(clasps his hands together)* See? Like that. Black is beautiful. Remember? Now, I'm gonna teach you something else. United...come on now. Come on – first I say it...then you say it. United we stand...

HAMBONE. United we stand....

STERLING. Divided we fall.

HAMBONE. Divided we fall.

STERLING. Yeah, that's right. See? You can do it! United we stand...divided we fall. I learned that in the penitentiary. You ever been in the penitentiary?

(HAMBONE *looks at him.* STERLING *suddenly shouts:*)

I want my ham!

HAMBONE. I want my ham!

STERLING. I want my ham!

HAMBONE. I want my ham!

STERLING. I want my ham!

HAMBONE. I want my ham!

STERLING. Malcolm lives!

HAMBONE. I want my ham!

STERLING. Malcolm lives!

HAMBONE. I want my ham!

STERLING. Malcolm lives!

HAMBONE. I want my ham!

(**MEMPHIS** *enters.*)

STERLING. Malcolm lives!

HAMBONE. I want my ham!

STERLING. Malcolm lives!

HAMBONE. I want my ham!

MEMPHIS. Stop all the hollering in here! This a business. Risa…

HAMBONE. I want my ham!

MEMPHIS. Stop all that hollering! Risa!

RISA. What?

MEMPHIS. What's all this hollering in here? You supposed to be running a business. This ain't no schoolyard! *(to* **STERLING***)* Go on outside if you wanna holler. Take that out on the street and holler all you want.

STERLING. We was just having some fun. Say Memphis, you wanna buy some gas? I got five gallon of gas I found in the alley down there off of Centre. Let you have it for two dollars.

MEMPHIS. I got gas.

STERLING. That gas you got ain't gonna last forever. I'll carry it out there and put it in your car if you want. It ain't gonna cost but two dollars. You know how much gas cost? Bean charge seventy-two cents a gallon. He charge three cent more than the white man.

(**MEMPHIS** *gives him two dollars.*)

MEMPHIS. Here. Bring the can back.

STERLING. I ain't said I was selling the can. That's two dollars if you wanna buy that. This a regulation United States Army gas can. Made with good metal and everything. Bullet probably bounce right off it.

MEMPHIS. I don't want to buy the can. I just say bring it back empty.

STERLING. Give me the key and let me drive it around the block a couple of times.

MEMPHIS. Nigger...give me back my two dollars!

STERLING. I was just playing around. I wouldn't even look right driving a Cadillac.

(*STERLING exits.*)

MEMPHIS. That boy ain't got good sense. I don't want all that hollering in here. Hambone paid you for these beans?

RISA. Naw.

MEMPHIS. That's sixty-five cent. You got sixty-five cent?

(**HAMBONE** *gives him three quarters.* **MEMPHIS** *goes to the register and rings it up. He takes* **HAMBONE**'s *change and slaps it down on the table in front of him.*)

Go on and finish your beans and get on where you going. Give him another muffin, Risa. (*to* **HAMBONE**) You eat that and get on with your business.

(*The phone rings.* **MEMPHIS** *answers it.*)

Hello? ...Wolf don't work here. (*slams down the phone*) Risa, Wolf been taking numbers out of here?

RISA. I don't know.

MEMPHIS. I told him about that. This ain't no number station. First thing you know they be raiding the place. Have my picture in the paper for racketeering. If there's one thing I can say, I ain't never had my picture in the paper.

(**STERLING** *enters with the gas can.*)

STERLING. Hey Risa...hold this for me.

MEMPHIS. You carry that right on back out there where you got it from – I don't want no part of it.

(**WOLF** *enters.*)

WOLF. How's everybody in here? I can smell them short ribs. Fix me up a plate, Risa.

RISA. They ain't done yet.

WOLF. Give me a bowl of beans. I'll be back for the short ribs. Hey Sterling...look here. *(takes out a brown paper bag)* You got twenty dollars?

STERLING. What for?

(**WOLF** *hands* **STERLING** *the bag. He looks inside.*)

WOLF. That's the best I can do. Tony Jackson say he want twenty dollars for it.

STERLING. I ain't got but two dollars and it ain't worth but fifteen.

WOLF. He say twenty. I'll loan it to you if you ain't got it.

STERLING. I can't pay you back till next week.

WOLF. That's all right. Pay me next week.

(**STERLING** *takes the bag and shoves it in his pants.*)

What you got there, Risa? That look like some of Prophet Samuel's flowers.

RISA. They ain't his no more.

STERLING. Let me spend my last two dollars. Give me two dollars on seven eighty-one straight. Seven eighty-one...right, Risa? If that come out me and Risa getting married. *(picks up his gas can and starts to exit)* Risa, fix me up a plate of them short ribs. I'll be right back.

(**STERLING** *exits.*)

MEMPHIS. I give that boy three weeks. You hear me, Holloway? Three weeks. And he gonna be laying over there across the street or back down there in the penitentiary. You watch. Three weeks.

(**RISA** *sets* **WOLF***'s beans in front of him. The phone rings and* **WOLF** *goes to answer it.* **MEMPHIS** *beats him to it.*)

Hello? ...Wolf don't work here!

WOLF. What you do that for, Memphis? That's my livelihood.

MEMPHIS. This my restaurant. I told you about taking numbers out of here. This is a legitimate business. This ain't no number station. Go on down to Seefus...give people the number down there. Risa...get these dishes cleaned up.

WOLF. Here you go, Risa...let me get out of here before I get in trouble. *(drops the money for his dinner on the counter)*

MEMPHIS. You gonna do more than get in trouble if you messing with me.

WOLF. See... I ain't said nothing to you now, Memphis. You starting something?

MEMPHIS. This my place, nigger! This my place. How you gonna have people call you at my place?

WOLF. I ain't told nobody to call me. People know I be here and they trying to catch me. I get messages everywhere I go. Nobody else don't say nothing about it.

MEMPHIS. Well, go on and get them, 'cause you ain't getting no more here.

(WOLF exits. MEMPHIS smells something.)

What's that burning? Risa?

(MEMPHIS crosses behind the counter.)

Risa, watch you don't burn these short ribs. You got the fire way up high. What you doing back there?

RISA. I'm getting the food ready.

MEMPHIS. That don't take all day. Them short ribs need some more water. Put some water in there.

(RISA goes to put some water in the short ribs.)

Turn the fire down and get on down to the store and get some cornmeal. Where's the cornmeal? How you gonna make muffins without cornmeal?

(WEST enters.)

Hey, West.

WEST. Somebody done busted out my window. A great big old six-foot piece of glass! People ain't got sense enough to walk through the door. Over there pushing and carrying on. Let me get some coffee, Risa. I don't care how many people be lined up there to see Prophet Samuel...he leaving my place tomorrow. I'm talking about a big piece of glass! Ain't no telling how much it cost to replace that.

RISA. You ought to put a board up there.

WEST. I ain't gonna put up no board. They better get out here with that piece of glass. I spent twelve years putting up board. I worked hard not to put up board. Let them cut a piece of glass and bring it out and bill me. There was a time when they wouldn't do that. When I was down there on Centre I couldn't get the windows fixed. The toilet break down it be two weeks before somebody come and fix it. When I built that over there I said that wasn't gonna happen. Something go wrong I call the man who built it and he come right out and take care of it. No, sweetheart, West ain't gonna put up no board.

MEMPHIS. I hear tell somebody tried to break in there.

WEST. Tried to come in through the basement window. Let me get a little sugar here, Risa. I hired Mason to sit over there tonight. I want to see them come in with him there.

HOLLOWAY. They be a fool to tangle with Mason and that twelve-gauge shotgun. The police sorry they had to retire him, as many niggers as he done shot.

WEST. Say Memphis, I told you what was gonna happen when you went down there. But you don't listen to nobody. They got it all stacked up against you before you walk through the door.

MEMPHIS. That's all right. I know how to deal with white folks. Ask Holloway. Down from where we come from you learn how to deal with white folks quick. It won't be the first time I bucked heads with white folks about my property.

WEST. I tell you what I do...you wanna be stubborn... I'll go ahead and give you twenty thousand for it.

MEMPHIS. You gonna give me twenty thousand?

WEST. We can go right on down to the bank now. I'll give you fifteen now and five thousand after I sell it to the city.

MEMPHIS. I knew there was a catch to it.

WEST. I can't give it all to you now You know I gotta leverage it with my other property. It's liable to be two or three years before I get my money. I'm fighting with the insurance company now about my two places that burned down. I got to wait and see how all that turns out. I'll give you the fifteen now and five later.

MEMPHIS. That's all right. I see what you doing. You gonna use me to leverage your property and string me out for five thousand while you collect the interest and settle up on your insurance till you get big money and then after you get it in your pocket in two or three years then you kick me out my little five thousand dollars. That ain't right. That ain't the way to do business.

WEST. That's the only way to do business. I'm trying to help you and quite naturally I got to look for every little advantage that I can get. You ought to be able to understand that.

MEMPHIS. I understand it. That's why I'm going downtown to the city and get my twenty-five thousand dollars. Just like I'm going back to Jackson and get my land one of these days. I still got the deed. They ran me out of there but I'm going back. I got me a piece of farm down there. Everybody said I was crazy to buy it 'cause it didn't have no water on it. They didn't know my grandaddy knew how to find water. If there was water anywhere under the ground he'd find it. He told me where to dig and I dug a well. Dug sixty feet down. You ain't got no idea how far that is. Took me six months hauling dirt out this little hole. Found me some water and made me a nice little crop.

MEMPHIS. *(cont.)* Jim Stovall, who I bought the land from, told me my deed say if I found any water the sale was null and void. Went down to the court to straighten it out and come to find out he had a bunch of these fellows get together to pick on me. He try to act like he ain't had nothing to do with it. They took and cut my mule's belly out while it standing there. Just took a knife and sliced it open. I stood there and watched them. They was laughing about it. I look and see where they got me covered. There's too many of them to fool around with. I didn't want to die. But I loved that old mule. Me and him had been through a lot together. He was a good old mule. Remind me of myself. He only do so much amount of work and that was it. He didn't mind working. He liked to get out there and exercise. Do anything you asked him. He didn't like you to half-work him. If you gonna work him…he want you to work him. Or else let him lay. He didn't like no stop-and-start work. That wasn't to his suiting. Don't tell him you gonna do one thing and then do something else. He'd lay down and tell you, "Goddamn it, make up your mind!" I used to take him down there and let him mate with Jimmy Hollis's mule. I figure I get mine, let him get his. A man like him a woman after a hard day's work. I stood there and watched them cut his belly open. He kinda reared back, took a few steps, and fell over. One of them reached down, grabbed hold of his dick, and cut that off. I stood there looking at them. I say, "Okay. I know the rules now. If you do that to something that ain't never done nothing to you…then I know what you would do to me. So I tell you what. You go on and get your laugh now. 'Cause if I get out of this alive I know how to play as good as anyone." Once I know the rules, whatever they are, I can play by them.

Went in there, saw the judge, and he say the deed was null and void. Now I got to walk home. I was looking for them to try something. But I didn't see nobody.

Got home and they had set fire to my crop. To get to my house I'd have to walk through fire. I wasn't ready to do that. I turned around and walked up the hill to Natchez. Called it a draw. Said I was going back. Got up there and got tied up with one of them Mississippi gals and one year led to two led to five. Then I come on up here in '36. But I'm going back one of these days.

(STERLING *enters.*)

STERLING. Say Mr. West, I was thinking, you know, I ain't never driven me no Cadillac. I figure everybody supposed to drive a Cadillac at least once before they die. A man got seven Cadillacs need somebody to drive them, right? You should see me drive. Can't nobody beat me driving. I drove a getaway car once. We got away, too. So, do you need any drivers?

WEST. No, I got everybody I need.

STERLING. If you ever need anybody just let me know. Okay? I done been in the penitentiary. I'll tell you that up front. I don't want to go back. I figure everybody should work at what they like to do. So I asked myself, "Sterling, what you like to do?" The closest I could come up with was I like to drive a Cadillac. So if you ever need anybody you think of me. Do you have to wash the cars if you drive them? I don't want to wash them without driving them. But if I could wash them seven at a time every day for about five dollars apiece I might do that. How long you reckon it take to do that? I don't reckon it take more than three hours. If you do a good job. I could do that for you.

WEST. Naw, I got somebody to wash my cars.

STERLING. I know. Every time I see them they be clean. Except for the grille. I could clean the grille better than that. You ought to tell them to get a little brush to scrub in them little spots with. It won't hurt the chrome none. Mr. Lewis taught me how to do that.

WEST. If I ever need anybody I'll let you know.

HOLLOWAY. Did you go back up there to see Aunt Ester?

STERLING. I went back up there they told me she was asleep.

HOLLOWAY. You give her a chance to get her rest, then you go on back up there. I'm going up and see her myself. West been up there. He don't like to tell nobody but he been up there.

WEST. I don't care who know. Yeah, I been up there.

MEMPHIS. You been up there, West?

WEST. Yeah, I went up there and saw her. I didn't take her to be no more than a hundred or so.

HOLLOWAY. Tell him when that was. Tell him how long that's been.

WEST. It's been twenty-two years. That don't mean she still alive. I ain't seen her in twenty-two years and she look like she was half-dead then. I can't imagine what she look like now.

HOLLOWAY. She look like she looked then. She wasn't but three hundred years old then. I don't reckon them twenty-two years make that much difference to her.

WEST. The oldest person I buried was Miss Sarah Degree and she was a hundred and twelve. I don't think nobody can live too much longer than that.

HOLLOWAY. You can go on back up and see her. She still there.

MEMPHIS. What you go up there for, West?

WEST. I went up there to see if my wife was in heaven. I done buried a whole lot of people, but she the first one I ever wondered about. See, people don't understand about death, but if you ever hear one of them coffin sounds you'd know. There ain't nothing like it. That coffin get to talking and you know that this here…this what we call life ain't nothing. You can blow it away with a blink of an eye. But death…you can't blow away death. It lasts forever. I didn't understand about it till my wife died. Before that it was just a job. Then when she died I come to understand it. You can live to be a hundred and fifty and you'll never have a greater moment than when you breathe your last breath. Ain't nothing you can do in life compared to it. See, right then you done something. You became a part of everything that come before. And that's a great thing. Ain't nothing you can do in life compared to that. So I heard about Aunt Ester and went to see if my wife was in heaven. I figure if anybody know she would.

MEMPHIS. What she tell you?

WEST. She told me to take and throw twenty dollars in the river and come back and see her. I thought she was crazy to tell you the truth. I didn't pay her no mind, I knew she was old, but I figure she had gotten too old.

HOLLOWAY. That's what your problem is. You don't want to do nothing for yourself. You want somebody else to do it for you. Aunt Ester don't work that way. She say you got to pull your part of the load. But you didn't want to do that. That's why you don't know. And it didn't cost you but twenty dollars.

WEST. I wasn't gonna throw my money in the river, nigger.

HOLLOWAY. That's why you don't know. You don't know what might have happened if you did that. If you had gone on back up there she might have told you.

WEST. I offered to give her the twenty dollars just for her time…but she wouldn't take it. Told me to throw it in the river. I'd rather see her with it than to see it at the bottom of the river. I just wasn't gonna do that with my money.

HOLLOWAY. That's why you don't know.

WEST. If it take throwing my money in the river to find out then I ain't never gonna know.

MEMPHIS. What you go up to see her about, Holloway? What happened when you threw your twenty dollars in?

HOLLOWAY. I went up there to see her 'cause I wanted to kill my grandfather. I went up there and got that feeling off me. I had to throw twenty dollars every week for a month. But I got it off me. He died from natural causes. Ask West...he buried him. He died in his sleep. That's why I knew it worked. 'Cause he died of natural death.

MEMPHIS. What you wanna kill your grandfather for?

HOLLOWAY. Now you getting in my business. Ask West if he ain't died a natural death. That's all you need to know.

MEMPHIS. I don't care nothing about your business. You the one brought it up. I ain't even know you had a grandfather.

HOLLOWAY. Had two of them. One on my mother's side and one on my father's side. One of them I never knew. The other one wasn't no good for nobody. That was the worse Negro I ever known. He think if it wasn't for white people there wouldn't be no daylight. If you let him tell it, God was a white man who had a big plantation in the sky and sat around drinking mint juleps and smoking Havana cigars. He couldn't wait to die to get up in heaven to pick cotton. If he overheard you might wanna go down and get you some extra meat out the white man's smokehouse...he'd run and tell him. He see you put a rabbit in your sack to weigh up with the cotton, he'd run and tell. The white man would give him a couple pounds of bacon. He'd bring that home and my grandmother would throw it out with the garbage. That's the kind of woman she was. I don't know how she got tied up with him. She used to curse the day she laid down with him. That rubbed off on me. I got a little older to where I could see what kind of man he was... I figure if he want to go to heaven to pick cotton, I'd help him. I got real serious about it. It stayed on me so didn't nobody want to be around me 'cause of the bad energy I was carrying. Couldn't keep me a woman. Seemed like nothing wouldn't work out for me. I went up to see Aunt Ester and got that bad energy off me. And it worked too. Ask West. He died in his sleep. Caught pneumonia and laid down and died. They wouldn't let him in the hospital 'cause he didn't have any insurance. He crawled up in the bed in my grandmother's house and laid there till he died. March 5, 1952. So can't nobody tell me nothing about Aunt Ester. I know what she can do for you.

WEST. Let me get on. Say Memphis, if you change your mind about the building, let me know.

(WEST *exits.*)

STERLING. I'm going back up there soon as I get some money. I'll throw twenty dollars in the river if it help me get a job.

HOLLOWAY. You go on back up there.

STERLING. Say, Memphis...you know how many people be down at the steel mill hanging around there at lunchtime? You ever seen that? Must be five or six hundred. I figure we could make some money selling chicken sandwiches. All you need is a little truck...have Risa fry up the chicken and I go over there and sell them. You ever thought about that? We could go in business together.

MEMPHIS. I'm in business already. You go on and get your truck and go on over there. Risa...get these dishes cleaned up.

STERLING. (*starting toward the door*) That all right...if that seven eighty-one come out I'll have me enough money I won't need to go in no business. If that seven eighty-one come out me and Risa gonna get married. Ain't that right, Risa?

(RISA *doesn't say anything.*)

She shy. She don't want to let everybody know. Hey Memphis, if I find some more gas I'll bring it on around. Okay?

(STERLING *exits.*)

MEMPHIS. I changed that, Holloway. I give him two weeks.

(*The lights go down on the scene.*)

Scene II

(The lights come up on the restaurant. **RISA** *sits on
a stool reading a magazine.* **HOLLOWAY** *enters.)*

HOLLOWAY. Risa, you seen Hambone today?

RISA. Naw, he ain't been in here.

HOLLOWAY. You know he wasn't over there this morning.
Lutz asked me about him.

RISA. He ain't been in here. Anybody know where he stay
at?

HOLLOWAY. He was staying up there on Arcena Street. He
stayed up there for the longest time. He ain't up there
no more. Nobody know where he stay at.

RISA. Maybe he just quit coming. He might have moved
to Homewood or East Liberty. Got tired of waiting on
Lutz to give him his ham.

HOLLOWAY. I ain't known him to miss a day in nine-and-a-
half years. He come and stand there even on Sunday
just in case Lutz show up. That don't sound like nobody
got tired of waiting.

*(***WOLF*** enters.)*

WOLF. Hey…Holloway. Did you see that out there this
morning? West was having a fit trying to bury Prophet
Samuel.

HOLLOWAY. Yeah, I was out there. They say the hearse was
at the cemetery and some of the cars hadn't even left
from in front of the funeral home.

WOLF. They had the boulevard backed up two miles.
People's cars overheating. They tried to block off the
street and let the cars go in two lanes, but the people
was arguing with the police and wouldn't let them do
it. They had helicopters flying all over the place.

RISA. Look like they had more people watching than was
in the funeral. They was lined up on both sides of the
street. Half of them was in here.

WOLF. I know. I couldn't get near the door. That was the biggest funeral West ever had.

HOLLOWAY. It wasn't as big as Patchneck Red's funeral. This wasn't nothing but Pittsburgh niggers. For Patchneck Red's funeral they came from Detroit, Cleveland, and all parts of Ohio and New Jersey. Youngstown... Newark...Jersey City. Come from West Virginia. They had eleven Cadillacs full of women come all the way from Vegas. People didn't leave the cemetery till the next morning. They was out there pouring whiskey on the grave...had two five-gallon buckets full of dice and fifty-eleven decks of cards they dumped in the grave with him. Prophet Samuel wasn't nothing like that. You find out anything about Hambone?

WOLF. I been asking around. Ain't nobody seen him. Last time anybody seen him was yesterday.

HOLLOWAY. Lutz say he ain't seen him either.

WOLF. How you doing, Risa? You lucky to see me today. If that six fifty-seven had come out I'd be in Atlanta right now.

HOLLOWAY. Who you know in Atlanta, Wolf?

WOLF. I got me a woman down there. Got two. Got one up on Jackson Hill and the other one stay on Lombard Street. One of them got four or five other men, but that's all right with me. All I got to do is call. All she got to do is hear my voice and she drop them other niggers. All she got to do is hear my voice and she come running. Any time of day or night.

HOLLOWAY. Well, why ain't you down there, then? You walking around here without a woman talking about you got two in Atlanta. Why ain't you there?

WOLF. I can't go down there unless I got some money. One of them think I'm a rich man. Last time she seen me I had six or seven hundred dollars in my pocket. Spent two hundred of it on her. She think I got that kind of money all the time. If that six fifty-seven had come out I'd been right there sitting on her doorstep. I had ten dollars straight on it. That's Harvey's number. He hit on that two or three times a year. I figured today might have been his lucky day.

HOLLOWAY. I see you and Memphis got in a little hassle yesterday.

WOLF. We all right. Memphis gets beside himself sometimes. See, he don't know he lucky I understand him. Without that understanding it be a different thing.

(MEMPHIS *enters.*)

HOLLOWAY. Hey, Memphis. You know Hambone didn't come today? You ain't seen him, have you?

MEMPHIS. Naw, I ain't seen him.

HOLLOWAY. That ain't like him not to show up.

MEMPHIS. Risa, get these dishes cleaned off the counter.

(MEMPHIS *and* WOLF *glare at each other.*)

HOLLOWAY. Hey Wolf, give me a dime on nine sixty-eight. I'm gonna keep playing it till it come out.

WOLF. I got to ask Memphis. Memphis, is it okay if I take Holloway's number? I mean, since this is a legitimate business and all.

MEMPHIS. I said I didn't want you using my phone, Wolf. You can twist it all out of shape if you want. I can't have them running in here raiding my place. I don't take no numbers out of here. Seem like you be able to understand that.

WOLF. I understand it. What you want, Holloway?

HOLLOWAY. Give me a dime on nine sixty-eight. Box it for a nickel.

(WOLF *writes down his number.*)

MEMPHIS. Give me a dollar on four seventy-eight.

WOLF. You know, Sterling hit for two dollars yesterday on that seven eighty-one? He ain't gonna like it none, but they cut the number. They cut it in half. They ain't paying but half of it. I don't know what it was…seem like every nigger in Pittsburgh played seven eighty-one.

Ain't nobody gonna like it, but he ain't gonna like it especially. I started to carry my pistol today, but I say, "Naw... I might kill somebody." Most people understand when they cut the numbers...but I don't know about Sterling. He got his own way of looking at things. Holloway, if you see him would you try and explain it to him that it ain't my fault 'cause I will go to the pawnshop and get my pistol. So if you could explain that to him before I see him I'd appreciate it. That way you be helping us both out.

HOLLOWAY. If I know him like I think I do, he gonna wanna know why everybody play his number instead of their own. Then he gonna come to understand that he don't care how many people played it...the Alberts still owe him all his money. And since you work for the Alberts, if you don't get him his money, then you all in cahoots, and the Alberts is splitting it with you, and you gonna buy a Cadillac next week with his money... therefore you gonna need your pistol. And if it go that way... West is gonna get a chance to bury one of you. If he go up there and mess with the Alberts, then West gonna have to bury him in a closed casket. Now... I'm sixty-five years old and I got that way by staying out of people's business, so no... I ain't gonna tell him nothing. If he come in here right now I'd walk out. Come back tomorrow and Risa will have to tell me what happened.

WOLF. Well, I ain't gonna pay him out my pocket. The hell with it. You right. I got to go to the pawnshop and get my pistol. Hey Risa, I'll be back. If Sterling comes, tell him I was looking to see him.

(*WOLF exits.*)

HOLLOWAY. I don't know why I play the numbers. The Alberts want all the advantages. They got six-hundred-to-one odds, but that ain't enough for them. If thirty or forty niggers get lucky enough to hit the numbers the same day, they don't even want them to enjoy their luck. They want to take that away from them. They don't say nothing about cutting the numbers when six thousand niggers guess wrong.

MEMPHIS. They been cutting numbers for the past hundred years. That's part of the game. You supposed to understand that when you play your money. If I was – *(spies the flyer on the wall)* What the hell this doing up here? *(tears it down and crumples it up)* I don't want this up in my place. I ain't putting no sanction on nothing like that. That's what the problem is now. All them niggers wanna do is have a rally. Soon as they finish with one rally they start planning for the next. They forget about what goes in between. You rally to spur you into action. When it comes time for action these niggers sit down and scratch their heads. They had that boy Begaboo. The police walked up and shot him in the head and them same niggers went down there to see the mayor. Raised all kind of hell. Trying to get the cop charged with murder. They raised hell for three weeks. After that it was business as usual. The only thing anybody remember is the funeral. That's the Sterling boy bringing that stuff in here. Something wrong with that boy. That boy ain't right. *(to* **RISA**) If I was you I'd stay away from him. He ain't gonna do nothing but end up right back down there in the penitentiary.

HOLLOWAY. You might be right. Now he done got him a gun. What he gonna do with it? A nigger with a gun is bad news. You can't even use the word "nigger" and "gun" in the same sentence. You say the word "gun" in the same sentence with the word "nigger" and you in trouble. The white man panic. Unless you say, "The policeman shot the nigger with his gun"…then that be all right. Other than that he panic. He ain't had nothing but guns for the last five hundred years…got the atomic bomb and everything. But you say the word "nigger" and "gun" in the same sentence and they'll try and arrest you. Accuse you of sabotage, disturbing the peace, inciting a riot, plotting to overthrow the government and anything else they can think of. You think I'm lying? You go down there and stand in front of the number two police station and say, "The niggers is tired of this mistreatment – they gonna get some guns," and see if they don't arrest you.

MEMPHIS. As young and as crazy as that boy is, he need to carry one.

(*STERLING enters.*)

STERLING. How you doing, Memphis? Risa… Wolf been in here?

RISA. He just left. He say he be back.

STERLING. I was out there watching them bury Prophet Samuel. Harvey gave me a ride to the cemetery. Was you over there, Risa? I was looking for you.

RISA. Everybody running over there to see him 'cause he dead. They didn't go see him when he was alive. He was right up there on Herron Avenue. They wasn't lining up there then.

STERLING. It be like that with everything. People don't care nothing about you till you dead. Then they walk around and tell everybody how well they knew you and that make them special for a day or two. You always have more followers when you dead than when you living.

RISA. That's what I'm saying. Prophet Samuel used to preach about hypocrites and that's what half them people is. If you be a hypocrite it don't count with God. He want you all the time. That's what Prophet Samuel say. God can look into your heart and tell. But see… I knew Prophet Samuel when he was living.

(*She hands* **STERLING** *a card.*)

STERLING. (*reading*) "This certifies that Risa Thomas is a member in good standing of the First African Congregational Kingdom, having duly paid all tithing… Signed, Prophet Samuel."

(*He hands her back the card.*)

STERLING. *(cont.)* I remember Prophet Samuel, but I ain't paid preachers or nothing like that no mind.

RISA. Prophet Samuel wasn't no preacher. He was a prophet like they have in the Bible. God sent him to help the colored people get justice.

MEMPHIS. The people ain't thinking about no justice when they lined up there. They thinking about money like Prophet Samuel. That's all he thought about. Justice come second. When God send you he pay your way. God ain't paid Prophet Samuel's way. The people paid Prophet Samuel's way hoping they get a financial blessing. You running up there giving him your little bit of change – what it get you? I wish I had three, four hundred people bringing me money every week. That be all the financial blessing I need.

RISA. That's 'cause you don't believe in nothing. Whatever Prophet Samuel prophesied, it come true.

STERLING. Did he say anything about these being the last days? That's what I believe. I believe the world coming to an end.

RISA. He said God was gonna send a sign. That's all he said about that. Said you would see it, but only the wise men would know what it meant.

STERLING. I be looking at the moon. Seem like it's getting closer and closer. You ever notice that? You look up and see if it ain't getting closer. Maybe that's what he meant by a sign. You look next time when the moon be full and see if it ain't getting closer. You look and then go right back in your house. I don't go outside when it's a full moon. There be at least three or four people killed that night. I believe the world coming to an end.

(**RISA** *exits into the back.*)

MEMPHIS. If it do be the end of the world, what you gonna do? You can't do nothing but go down with it. It's foolish to worry about something like that. Something you ain't got no control over. If these niggers spent half the time they spend worrying about stuff like that and more time trying to figure out how to get out of the situation they in..,they wouldn't have all the problems they got now.

STERLING. Soon as I find Wolf I ain't gonna have no more problems. *(shouting to* RISA*)* Hey Risa…if you see Wolf… tell him I'm looking for him. He knows what it's about.

*(*STERLING *exits.)*

MEMPHIS. *(calling)* Risa!

RISA. What?

MEMPHIS. Come here, woman. *(pause)* If you want your pay you better get out here.

*(*RISA *enters from the back.)*

I owe you forty-six dollars with the ten you took.

RISA. I don't owe you but seven.

MEMPHIS. You ain't counting the three dollars you got the other day to buy some hair grease. You ain't counting that.

RISA. I told you I put the three dollars back 'cause they ain't had the kind I wanted.

MEMPHIS. Well, write a note saying you put it back. How in the hell I'm supposed to know you put it back? Here…take this forty-nine dollars. I got some business to take care of… Don't forget to put the bread in the refrigerator when you lock up. Put the bread in the refrigerator and make sure you pull the shade down on the door. I got to go down to the courthouse in the morning… Make sure you got enough eggs before you leave out of here. Well, Holloway… I was talking to my lawyer…Joseph Bartoromo… I was talking to him on the phone. He said let him handle it. I ain't gonna let him handle it but so far. I told him like I tell you… I ain't going for no more draws…and I ain't taking a penny less than twenty-five thousand dollars.

(He starts to exit and stops at the door.)

What's that address?

HOLLOWAY. 1839 Wylie. In the back. Knock on the red door.

(*The lights go down on the scene.*)

Scene III

(The lights come up on RISA *and* HOLLOWAY.
WOLF *sits at the table doing his bookkeeping.* RISA
is sweeping. It is later the same day.)

HOLLOWAY. He was staying up there on Herron Avenue.
They found him up there today. His landlady found
him. He just laid down across the bed with his clothes
on and died. Say he died real peaceful. West went
down to the morgue to get him...he got some kind
of contract with the welfare and they called him up.
Hambone ain't had no people. Most anybody know
about him is he come from Alabama. Don't nobody
even know his right name.

RISA. That's a shame. Lutz gonna rot in hell.

WOLF. Lutz ain't thinking about no hell. All he thinking
about is his ham.

HOLLOWAY. I went up there and told him about it 'cause
he asked me to let him know what I found out. He
didn't say nothing. He just looked at me.

*(RISA *accidentally sweeps* WOLF*'s feet.)*

WOLF. Don't sweep me with that broom, girl. Ain't your
mama never taught you nothing?

RISA. Well, move your feet out the way then.

WOLF. You sweep me with that broom and I'll end up in
jail.

HOLLOWAY. That's what's wrong with half these niggers
now. They don't know what causes their trouble. They
around here breaking mirrors, opening umbrellas in
the house, and everything else.

WOLF. Come on, Risa!

RISA. Move your feet then, Wolf! You be gone to jail twice
you don't move your feet.

(She sweeps him again.)

WOLF. Hey, Risa. Come on, now! *(gets up and gathers his papers)* A man can't get no peace around here. If you see Sterling, tell him I'm looking for him. Tell him to wait here, I'll be back.

(**WOLF** *exits.*)

HOLLOWAY. A man was driving a truck…hauling a whole truck full of mirrors…lost the brakes and ran into a telephone pole. He wasn't hurt or nothing. He looked back there and saw all them mirrors broke…he was staring at two hundred years of bad luck. They had to carry him away in a straitjacket.

(**WEST** *enters.*)

Hey West… I see you finally got Prophet Samuel buried.

WEST. Yeah… I got him in the ground and turned around and went down there and got Hambone. It don't never stop. Time you bury one nigger you got to go get another. Man had so many scars on his body… I ain't never seen nothing like that. All on his back, his chest…his legs. I'm gonna lay him out tomorrow and bury him on Saturday.

RISA. You ought to lay him out in a nice casket. I hate to see people laid out in them welfare caskets.

WEST. That's a poor man's casket. What you call a pauper's casket. He wouldn't look right laying in a bronze or silver casket.

RISA. I hate to see him in a welfare casket. Like his life ain't meant nothing. How much one of them other caskets cost?

WEST. You talking about a seven-hundred-dollar difference. The welfare don't pay but three hundred and fifty dollars. That don't even cover laying him out. I'm laying him out for free. I'm gonna lay him out for two hours tomorrow and take him on out there and bury him. You talking about a bronze casket you talking about seven hundred dollars. At least.

RISA. Ain't you got some other caskets over there?

WEST. I don't get them for free, woman. I call the company and order the casket, they send me the bill. We talking about a seven-hundred-dollar difference.

RISA. I wish I had seven hundred dollars to give you. I'd lay him out in a gold casket.

WEST. Now you talking about a seventeen-hundred-dollar difference. People don't understand. I got overhead. I got seven cars I got to keep up. Got supplies I got to order. How much you think that embalming fluid cost? I got all kinds of bills. People owe me money and won't pay me. It ain't all like everybody think with Mr. West.

RISA. I ain't said nothing about that.

WEST. You talking about why don't I lay him out in a different casket. That three hundred and fifty dollars barely cover my expenses. You can't put nobody in the ground for three hundred and fifty dollars no more. I bury him in a different casket I'm out seven hundred dollars. I try to tell these niggers to keep up their insurance.

(STERLING enters.)

RISA. Sterling, Wolf was looking for you.

STERLING. Naw, he ain't. I'm looking for him. Nigger owe me twelve hundred dollars. Come on, let's go to Vegas. I got me a grubstake, I might get lucky. These niggers ain't got no money around here. Come on...take off that apron. How you doing, Mr. West?

WEST. Fine.

STERLING. Say, Mr. West...you ever been to Vegas? You ought to let me take you to Vegas and teach you how to gamble. We can make us some money.

WEST. I was gambling before you was born. Give me some sugar, Risa. I ran two or three crap games. Sold bootleg liquor and ran numbers too. The only thing you get out of that is an early grave. I know. I seen it happening. I looked up one day and so many people was dying from that fast life I figured I could make me some money burying them and live a long life too. I figured

I could make a living from it. I didn't know I was gonna
get rich. I found out life's hard but it ain't impossible.

STERLING. That's what I figure. I get my money from
Wolf...get in one of them white folks' crap games it
be impossible to stop me. I'm gonna get me two or
three Cadillacs like you. Get Risa to be my woman and
I'll be all right. That's all a man need is a pocketful
of money, a Cadillac and a good woman. That's all he
need on the surface. I ain't gonna talk about that other
part of satisfaction. But I got sense enough to know
it's there. I know if you get the surface it don't mean
nothing unless you got the other. I know that, Mr. West.
Sometimes I think I'll just take the woman part. And
then sometimes that don't seem like it's enough.

WEST. That's 'cause you walking around here with a ten-
gallon bucket. Somebody put a little cupful in and you
get mad 'cause it's empty. You can't go through life
carrying a ten-gallon bucket. Get you a little cup. That's
all you need. Get you a little cup and somebody put
a little bit in and it's half full. That ten-gallon bucket
ain't never gonna be full. Carry you a little cup through
life and you'll never be disappointed. I'll tell you what
my daddy told me. I was a young man just finding
my way through life. I told him I wanted to find me
a woman and go away and get me a ranch and raise
horses like my grandaddy. I was still waiting around to
find the woman. He told me to get the ranch first and
the woman would come. And he was right. I never did
get me the ranch, but he was right.

STERLING. That's what I'm gonna do, Mr. West. You hear
that, Risa? Soon as I get my money we going to Vegas
and I'm gonna get me enough money to buy us a
ranch. You like horses? I ain't never seen a real horse.
I wouldn't know how to act around one. But if that's
what it takes to get a woman like you I'm willing to do
that. What's the matter? Don't you wanna go to Vegas
with me?

RISA. Go on, Sterling, I don't feel like playing. (to WEST) Ain't you got no other kind of metal casket over there? What about one of them copper caskets?

WEST. The government don't pay but three hundred and fifty dollars, woman! I'm doing him a favor laying him out. How you expect me to meet my expenses? If I laid everybody out in a bronze casket at my expense I'd be out of business.

RISA. I ain't talking about everybody. I'm talking about Hambone.

WEST. Insurance don't cost but two dollars a month. I try to tell people that.

STERLING. Hambone dead? Risa... Hambone dead?

RISA. They found him this morning laying across his bed

> (STERLING *is thrown for a moment, but recovers quickly.*)

STERLING. That don't surprise me. Don't nothing surprise me no more.

> (WOLF *enters.*)

Hey Wolf... Just the man I want to see. I need my money. Me and Risa getting married and Reverend Flowers want fifty dollars... The cake man want fifty dollars... The jewelry man want two hundred dollars. Hey, Risa...you want to invite Wolf? She say yeah. We ain't set the date yet...but we let you know. Where's my money, nigger? You got my money?

WOLF. Look, Sterling...it ain't my fault...but they cut the number. They cut it in half. They ain't paying but six hundred dollars.

STERLING. I'm like Joe Louis. They cut the odds on Joe Louis all the time. That seven eighty-one was like a knockout punch. I knew it was gonna hit. I'm going up and tell the Alberts that seven eighty-one don't hit like a forty-five. Mr. West, you don't bury white people, do you? That's all right. I ain't gonna kill nobody. I'll just put them in a wheelchair. *(to* WOLF*)* And I'm gonna start with you if you don't give me my twelve hundred dollars.

WOLF. I'm gonna tell you one more time, Sterling. I ain't had nothing to do with it. I know you mad. Everybody mad. They mad out in East Liberty. People in Beltzhoover… Everybody all up and down the avenue mad. I ain't had nothing to do with it. If it was up to me I'd pay everybody what they due. This is a job to me. That little bit they pay me ain't worth all that. They call me say "Wolf, the number's cut in half." I say "Okay." That's the way that go. The best I can say is you lucky they didn't cut it seven ways.

STERLING. Naw…naw, what you telling me is me and Risa got to postpone our getting married.

RISA. I ain't said nothing about getting married. Don't be telling everybody that. Wolf don't pay him no mind about that.

STERLING. See what I mean? Risa done changed her mind. I'm going up and see the Alberts, see if they change theirs. Give me my six hundred dollars, nigger.

(WOLF *pays him the money.*)

I'm going up there and give it back to them. See Old Man Albert himself. Let him know an airplane can fall on his head.

(STERLING *starts to exit.*)

WOLF. Don't do that, Sterling. Them people don't play.

STERLING. If I don't play…that mean there can't be no game. I'm going up there and carry me a big sign say "Game Canceled." See? 'Cause I don't play either.

(STERLING *exits.*)

RISA. *(calling after him)* Sterling!

(The lights go down on the scene.)

Scene IV

*(The lights come up on the restaurant. RISA is
sweeping the floor. STERLING enters.)*

STERLING. I come by to see if you wanna go to the rally. *(He
doesn't get a response.)* It done started already but I figure
we won't be too late.

RISA. You left out of here talking about you was gonna see
the Alberts... We didn't know if we was gonna see you
again.

STERLING. I didn't know it mattered to nobody. I heard
you calling me. What you calling after me for?

RISA. I just didn't want to see you get killed.

STERLING. I went up there to see Old Man Albert. He
sitting up there with four or five bodyguards. They let
me in to see him and I told him to give me back my
two dollars. Said I was calling off the bet. He gave me
the two dollars and asked me for his six hundred back.
I told him no. Told him I was gonna keep that. That
way I have something that belong to him for a change.
He just looked at me funny and told me to leave the
same way I had come in. Told one of his bodyguards to
show me the door. I left out of there and was walking
by Aunt Ester's. I saw the light on and I figure she
might be up, so I stopped to see her. They led me into
the hallway and then through some curtains into this
room...and she was just sitting there. I talked to her a
long while. Told her my whole life story. She real nice.
Ain't nobody ever talk to me like that. "I cannot swim
does not walk by the lakeside." It took me a while to
figure out what she meant. Told me, "Make better what
you have and you have best." Then she wrote down
something on a piece of paper, put it in a little enve-
lope, told me to put it in my shoe and walk around on
it for three days. I asked her how much I owed her. She
told me to take twenty dollars and throw it in the river.
Say she get it. She had this look about her real calm

and sweet like. I asked her how old she was. She say she was three hundred and forty-nine years old. Holloway had it wrong. I figured anybody that old know what she talking about. I took twenty dollars and carried it down there. Didn't even think about it. I just took and threw it in the river. I'm gonna wait them three days and see what happen. You ought to go up there and see her. She a real nice old lady. She say yeah, you the one God sent when he told me he couldn't send no angel.

RISA. Sterling, you crazy.

STERLING. I figure me and you get us a nice little old place... Ain't you tired of sleeping by yourself? I am.

RISA. Naw, I'm just fine taking care of me.

STERLING. You ain't got to take care of you...let me do that. I'll take care of you real good. *(singing:)*
WAKE UP, PRETTY MAMA
SEE WHAT I GOT FOR YOU
I GOT EVERYTHING
SET YOUR POOR HEART AT EASE
I GOT EVERYTHING FOR YOU, WOMAN.
I GOT A LIST OF THINGS
LONG AS MY RIGHT ARM.

RISA. Naw, that's all right.

STERLING. Woman, you everything a man need. Know how to cook...pay nice attention to yourself...except for those legs. You ought not to have done that. What you do that for anyway?

RISA. You wouldn't understand, Sterling.

STERLING. You be surprised... I got good understanding. That's what Aunt Ester told me. She looked at me and say, "I like to work with people like you 'cause you got good understanding." She say that before I could say anything to her. She just looked at me and said that. Now why can't you do that?

RISA. What you looking at my legs for anyway?

STERLING. That's part of life, woman. You don't think I'm not gonna look at them? Even if you tried to make

them ugly. So you wanted to have ugly legs...you got
them. Now what? I done looked at your legs, your hips,
your titties, and everything else. Now what? I don't care
if you got scars on your legs.

RISA. That's why I did it. To make them ugly.

STERLING. You did a good job. You and God both. He
made them pretty and you made them ugly. You both
got what you wanted. Now why can't I get what I want?

RISA. That's what the problem is.

STERLING. I know that's a problem. I'm trying to solve it.

RISA. You just want what everybody else want.

STERLING. Risa...you in the world, baby. You a woman in
the world. You here like everybody else. You got to
make the best of it. Quite naturally when men see you
with that big ass and them pretty legs they gonna try
and talk you into a bed somewhere. That's common
sense. They be less than a man if they didn't. Ain't no
sense in you getting upset about that. You ought to take
it as a compliment. All you got to do is say no and keep
on stepping.

RISA. That just what I done.

STERLING. I know that. Been telling me no since I met you.
By rights I should be talking to somebody else. I tried
that. But I was talking to her and thinking of you. So
I come on back.

RISA. You ain't got no job. You going back to the
penitentiary. I don't want to be tied up with nobody
I got to be worrying is they gonna rob another bank or
something.

STERLING. When I was living with Mrs. Johnson before
she died I used to watch her husband. He get up every
morning at six o'clock. Sunday too. Six-thirty he out
the door. Now...he ain't coming back till ten o'clock
at night. He going down to J&L and lift hundred-
pound slabs of steel till three o'clock. Then he going
over after they close the fish market and clean up over
there. Now what he got? He got six kids of his own,

not to mention me. He got a raggedy house with some beat-up furniture. Can't buy no house 'cause he can't get a loan. Now that sound like a hardworking man. Good. Clean. Honest. Upright. He work thirty years at the mill and ain't even got a union card. You got to work six months straight. They lay him off for two weeks every five and a half months. He got to call the police after he clean up the fish market so they can let him out of the building. Make sure he don't steal anything. What they got? Two pound of catfish? There got to be something else. I ain't sure I want to do all that.

RISA. You got to do something .

STERLING. Okay. Okay. If you don't want to get married and have babies and all that...then can we be cousins? Can we be kissing cousins? How's that?

> (He has cornered her. RISA pushes him away.)

RISA. Go on, Sterling...leave me alone now.

STERLING. Risa, baby...

RISA. What?

STERLING. I ain't never met no woman like you.

RISA. I ain't met no man like you either. But that don't mean I'm gonna get tied up with you. You'll never have me sitting and worrying what you gonna do next.

STERLING. Well, come on and go to the rally with me.

RISA. I ain't going to no rally. You can just go on by yourself.

> (RISA goes over to the jukebox and puts in a quarter. "Take a Look" by Aretha Franklin* begins to play.)

STERLING. When did that get fixed?

RISA. Today.

STERLING. (hesitant) You wanna dance?

RISA. Yeah.

---

*See Music Use Note on Copyright Page

(They begin to dance. **STERLING** *kisses her lightly.)*

STERLING. How's that? You wanna be kissing cousins? *(kisses her passionately)* Goddamn, baby!

RISA. Sterling.

STERLING. I didn't know it was gonna be like this. You can be my first cousin.

RISA. *(between kisses)* I wanna be your only cousin.

STERLING. That too.

*(***STERLING*** *kisses her as the lights go down on the scene.)*

Scene V

(The lights come up on the restaurant. The menu board reads: "Funeral for Hambone, Saturday, One o'clock." **HOLLOWAY** *sits in a booth.* **RISA** *is cooking.* **STERLING** *stands looking out the window.)*

HOLLOWAY. That's all you got. You got love and you got death. Death will find you...it's up to you to find love. That's where most people fall down at. Death got room for everybody. Love pick and choose. Now, most people won't admit that. They tell you they love this one and that one. Most don't even love their mother. You can see that by the way they treat her. But they'll tell you anything. But they got to know in their heart. I believe West loved his wife. And Bubba Boy loved his woman. Them's the only two people I can say found love. The rest of us play at it. That's 'cause love cost. Love got a price to it. Everybody don't want to pay. They put it on credit. Time it come due they got it on credit somewhere else. That's the way I see the world. That's what I done learned all these years.

*(**WOLF** enters.)*

WOLF. It look like Hong Kong out there. I didn't know there was that many niggers in Pittsburgh. If you drive by you'd swear didn't nobody have no home. They all out there on the street.

HOLLOWAY. The people out there looking for opportunity. Whatever's out there in the way of opportunity sooner or later it's got to pass through. You can't find out what's out there sitting at home. Why ain't you home? Talking about the people. You just come in from out there.

WOLF. I got business to take care of. I can't take care of it sitting at home.

HOLLOWAY. That's what I'm trying to tell you. You can't separate yourself from everybody else. The people out there trying to figure out how they gonna eat. It's day off on the plantation. They waiting for the white man to call them back to work.

WOLF. I went over there to see Hambone. West got him laid out real nice. He look like he sleeping. You been over, Sterling?

STERLING. I just left from over there.

WOLF. Don't he look real nice and peaceful? Look like he sleeping.

STERLING. He look like he dead to me. I sat there a while. I signed the book. Ain't but three or four people signed it.

WOLF. I signed it. I see Holloway signed it. Risa, you going over?

RISA. No... I don't want to see him like that.

WOLF. I saw you all down at the rally last night. Wasn't that something? Everybody was down there. Even the niggers that swear up and down on two stacks of Bibles that they ain't black...they was down there. Ain't had but five hundred chairs and three thousand people. Wasn't no fight or nothing. It was real nice.

STERLING. The police was down there taking people's pictures.

WOLF. I seen that. Wasn't that something? They don't go out there where the white folks at and take their pictures.

STERLING. I smiled when they took mine.

WOLF. I was standing down there watching that drugstore. It's still smoking from the fire last night. They ain't put it out yet. They must have had every fire truck in the world down there. Did you all see that? It wasn't nothing but a little old drugstore. Had ten, eleven fire trucks and near about a hundred police. Say it started in the back by the alley. A couple of people seen some of them Black Power niggers around there.

HOLLOWAY. That ain't nothing but talk. Everybody know the man burned down his own store so he could get the insurance. That's the only way he get anything out of it. If he pack up and leave he don't get nothing. This way he get paid for everything...all his stock... his building...everything. That's the best way to sell a business don't nobody want to buy. Sell it to the insurance company. All them niggers standing down there watching the fire...they don't know...but somebody's going to jail. The police got to snatch one of them. That way the insurance company pay quicker. Meyer's gonna walk away with two hundred thousand dollars and somebody going to jail for three years. See if I ain't right. You watch over the next two or three days and see if they don't arrest somebody as he walking by there. Meyer's gonna be down there in Florida playing golf and laying on the beach...and the fire inspector's gonna be right there with him. That's the way it works in America.

WOLF. You right about that. It's hard to live in America. Did you all hear where Petey Brown killed his old lady last night? Caught her in the Ellis Hotel with his best friend. Killed him too. That's why I don't have no one woman. When I die every woman in Pittsburgh gonna cry. They ain't gonna know what to do with themselves. My woman come and told me she had another man. I told her say "All right, baby but he can't hear and he can't see. He can't see like I do. You got to be able to pull a whole lot of boxcars to keep up with me." I'm like Prophet Samuel...if a man can get him seven women... if he can find seven women want to be with him... let him have them seven and one or two more. Seven women wanna lay down with him must see something they like. Hell, it's hard to get one, let alone seven. It's hard to get one you can trust that far. See, when you lay down with her, you trusting her with your life. You lay down you got to close your eyes. It wouldn't be nothing for somebody to walk up and slit your throat. That's why you lock the door at night. You lock the door and it be just you and her. That's a whole lot of trust there.

If I had that I wouldn't give it up for nothing. Other than that when I die every woman in Pittsburgh gonna cry.

(WEST *enters.*)

HOLLOWAY. Hey, West.

WOLF. Mr. West himself!

WEST. How you doing, Holloway? Hey Risa, give me a cup of coffee. Memphis ain't come back yet?

HOLLOWAY. I hope he didn't go down there and act a fool to where they had to lock him up. The courthouse been closed.

STERLING. Say Mr. West... I just wanna tell you...you did a good job on Hambone. I just wanna tell you that.

WEST. I got him laid out there for two hours tonight...just in case anybody wanna see him...then I'm gonna take him on out there and bury him tomorrow. Lutz come by to see him after he closed his store.

RISA. Lutz gonna rot in hell.

WOLF. Lutz gonna go to hell with a ham under each arm.

RISA. You want some coffee, Sterling?

STERLING. Yeah, give me a cup.

WEST. Let me get some sugar, Risa.

HOLLOWAY. Things done quieted down over there now with Prophet Samuel gone.

WEST. It took seven hours to bury him.

HOLLOWAY. Hey West, tell him...that wasn't nothing like Patchneck Red.

WEST. I ain't never seen nothing like that. The way them people carried on...it was sinful. I buried that boy Begaboo but it wasn't nothing like that. There was just as many people, but they was respectful. Them niggers come to bury Patchneck Red act like it was a party.

STERLING. Here's your twenty dollars, Wolf. Hey Risa... hold this for me.

RISA. What's that?

STERLING. That's my money. All five hundred and sixty-two dollars of it. Hold it for me… I'll be right back.

(**STERLING** *exits.*)

WOLF. Risa, what's going on with you and Sterling? Something going on. Don't get me wrong now, I ain't said nothing wrong with it. You know me. I live and let live. I think it's nice.

RISA. Wolf, ain't nobody paying you no mind.

WOLF. Naw, Sterling's all right with me. He act kind of crazy sometime. But he all right with me. I think it's nice.

(**MEMPHIS** *enters, singing. He has been drinking.*)

MEMPHIS.

WE DON'T CARE WHAT MAMA DON'T ALLOW
WE GONNA BARRELHOUSE ANYHOW.

Hey… Hey… Holloway. You know the Brass Rail down there by the courthouse? Man…they got a barmaid down there you can stand up right next to Risa. She gonna wait on me till I come back. She down there now. I told her I'll be back. She get off at seven o'clock. I left the courthouse, stopped down there and got me a few drinks. Hey…hey…Risa, fix me something to eat. Holloway… I took that twenty dollars and threw it in the river…right down there in the Monongahela River… I went and stood on the Brady Street Bridge… I didn't just let it drop. I took and tied a rock around it and threw it…just like Aunt Ester say. She told me if I do that everything be all right. And she was right too. She told me, "If you can't fight the fire, don't mess with it." Only I'm ready to fight it now. Hey West…look here… I went down there to the courthouse ready to fight for that twenty-five thousand dollars I want for my property. I wasn't taking no fifteen. I wasn't taking no twenty. I want twenty-five thousand. They told me, "Well, Mr. Lee…we got a clause, and the city is prepared to put into motion" – that's the part I like, "prepared to put into motion" – "the securing of your property at 1621 Wylie Avenue" – they had the address right and everything – "for the sum of thirty-five thousand dollars." I liked to fell over. The lawyer standing there, he know I'm mad and he ready to fight it. I told him, "Don't you say a word. Don't you open your mouth." Thirty-five thousand dollars! I started to go up and tell my wife. She up there. She up there at the house. She come back to get her things and ended up staying. I moved out. She moved back in and I moved out. Told her I had something to do and if she be there when I get back – if I get back – then we can sit down and talk. You know what I'm gonna do? Aunt Ester clued me on this one. I went up there and told her my whole life story. She say "If you drop the ball, you got to go back and pick it up. Ain't no need in keeping running, 'cause if you get to the end zone it ain't gonna be a touchdown." She didn't say it in them words but that's what she meant. Told me… "You got to go back and pick up the ball." That's what I'm gonna do. I'm going back to Jackson and see Stovall. If he ain't there, then I'm gonna see his son. He enjoying his daddy's benefits he got to carry his daddy's weight. I'm going on back up to Jackson and pick up the ball.

(He notices the sign on the menu board.)

"Funeral for Hambone, Saturday, One o'clock." Hambone dead? He dead?

RISA. He died in his sleep.

MEMPHIS. Lutz never did give him his ham, did he? I always figured one day Lutz would break down and give it to him. Either that or he'd take it.

*(He mimics **HAMBONE**:)*

He gonna give me my ham. He gonna give me my ham. I want my ham.

(He is in pain, wounded by all the cruel and cold ironies of life. He reaches into his pocket.)

Risa…take this fifty dollars and get some flowers. *(gives her some money)* Get him a big bunch. Put on there where it say who it's from…say it's from everybody…everybody who ever dropped the ball and went back to pick it up. Risa, where's my plate? I got to eat something. I'm going on back down there to the Brass Rail. Me and… me and… I forget her name…we gonna celebrate. You believe that, Holloway? Hey, West…thirty-five thousand dollars. When I get back…if I get back from seeing Stovall… I'm gonna open me up a big restaurant right down there on Centre Avenue. I'm gonna need two or three cooks and seven or eight waitresses. I'm gonna fix it up real nice. Gonna put me a jukebox…fix it so the lights go up and down and everything.

> *(The sound of glass breaking and a burglar alarm is heard.)*

Hell, I might even put a carpet on the floor. Put little chandeliers…get me a neon sign. I'm talking about a big neon. You be able to see it from Herron Avenue. I'm gonna put everything on the menu. Short ribs. Bar-B-Que… I might have me a little takeout on the side… put in a separate entrance…

> *(**STERLING** enters, carrying a large ham. He is bleeding from his face and his hands. He grins and lays the ham on the counter.)*

STERLING. Say Mr. West…that's for Hambone's casket.

> *(The lights fade to black.)*

End of Play

August Wilson

(April 27, 1945 – October 2, 2005)

August Wilson authored *Gem of the Ocean, Joe Turner's Come and Gone, Ma Rainey's Black Bottom, The Piano Lesson, Seven Guitars, Fences, Two Trains Running, Jitney, King Hedley II* and *Radio Golf.* These works explore the heritage and experience of African Americans, decade by decade, over the course of the twentieth century. Mr. Wilson's plays have been produced at regional theaters across the country, on Broadway and throughout the world. In 2003, Mr. Wilson made his professional stage debut in his one-man show *How I Learned What I Learned.*

Mr. Wilson's work garnered many awards, including the Pulitzer Prize for *Fences* (1987) and *The Piano Lesson* (1990); a Tony Award for *Fences*; Great Britain's Olivier Award for *Jitney*; and eight New York Drama Critics Circle awards for *Ma Rainey's Black Bottom, Fences, Joe Turner's Come and Gone, The Piano Lesson, Two Trains Running, Seven Guitars, Jitney* and *Radio Golf.* Additionally, the cast recording of *Ma Rainey's Black Bottom* received a 1985 Grammy Award, and Mr. Wilson received a 1995 Emmy Award nomination for his screenplay adaptation of *The Piano Lesson.* Mr. Wilson's early works include the one-act plays: *The Janitor, Recycle, The Coldest Day of the Year, Malcolm X, The Homecoming* and the musical satire *Black Bart and the Sacred Hills.*

Mr. Wilson received many fellowships and awards, including Rockefeller and Guggenheim fellowships in playwriting, the Whiting Writers Award and the 2003 Heinz Award. He was awarded a 1999 National Humanities Medal by the President of the United States, and received numerous honorary degrees from colleges and universities, as well as the only high school diploma ever issued by the Carnegie Library of Pittsburgh.

He was an alumnus of New Dramatists, a member of the American Academy of Arts and Sciences, a 1995 inductee into the American Academy of Arts and Letters, and on October 16, 2005, Broadway renamed the theater located at 245 West 52nd Street: The August Wilson Theatre. In 2007, he was posthumously inducted into the Theater Hall of Fame.

Mr. Wilson was born and raised in the Hill District of Pittsburgh, and lived in Seattle at the time of his death. He is survived by two daughters, Sakina Ansari and Azula Carmen Wilson, and his wife, costume designer Constanza Romero.

ideas:

- up rooted design
    - hyper realistic, but edges are being
      pulled and dragged away
    - boards cut off, jagged edges
    - maybe half present furniture
        - counter fading away, half a
          jukebox, etc.

- vivid colors like in Do the Right Thing
- clock